Losing My Mind-Gaining My Faith

By

Mary Ellen Cornelison

CREDITS

Editor: Jesse Sommer

Editor: Kevin Schneider

Book Designer: Leanore Elliott

copyright© 2024 **Mary Ellen Cornelison**

TABLE OF CONTENTS

- Acknowledgements……………..**Page 5**
- Dedication……………………………**Page 6**
- Book Description…………………**Page 7**
- Into The Abyss………………….**Page 9**
- Chapter One……………………..**Page 14**
- Chapter Two…………………….**Page 18**
- Chapter Three………………….**Page 23**
- Chapter Four…………………….**Page 28**
- Chapter Five…………………….**Page 33**
- Chapter Six……………………….**Page 40**
- Chapter Seven…………………**Page 45**
- Chapter Eight………………….**Page 52**
- Chapter Nine…………………..**Page 57**
- Chapter Ten……………………**Page 65**
- Chapter Eleven……………….**Page 73**
- Chapter Twelve……………….**Page 80**
- Chapter Thirteen………………**Page 87**

- Chapter Fourteen...................**Page 105**
- Chapter Fifteen......................**Page 112**
- Chapter Sixteen....................**Page 124**
- Chapter Seventeen..............**Page 132**
- Chapter Eighteen.................**Page 149**
- Chapter Nineteen................**Page 154**
- Chapter Twenty...................**Page 169**
- Chapter Twenty-One..........**Page 198**
- About The Author...............**Page 207**

Acknowledgements

I would like to extend my heartfelt gratitude to my dear friend, Victoria Sellers, for her unwavering support of my endeavors and her dedication to spreading the joy of reading. I have a passion for helping those in need learn to read because I grew up struggling with dyslexia my whole childhood. I struggled in school with not much help back then. I have overcome that challenge and am now writing books. Victoria has my passion for literacy programs. As a widow, Victoria has embraced this mission so close to her heart: to promote literacy in honor of her late husband and soulmate, Tim Sellers. Tim was a passionate reader who once amassed an impressive collection of over 5,000 books. Inspired by his legacy, Victoria initiated the creation of a single tiny library in his memory. This tiny library holds new and used donated books so anyone in the community walking by can grab a book and replace it with one they have already read.

This humble project has since blossomed into a remarkable network of 27 tiny libraries and one tiny art gallery along the picturesque Highway 30A corridor on the beautiful Emerald Coast of Florida. Stay tuned for Victoria's very own compelling story of love, heartbreak, and resilience, which serves as a testament to the power of literature and community. Follow her journey at @30ATinyLibrary.

Dedication

I have to dedicate this book to my best friend and sister, Destin Lowery. Destin has been there with me through my darkest times to pray for me and talk me off of the ledge. She is a true testament of unwavering love and commitment of sisterhood. I couldn't have made most of my "Boss Bitch" movements without her by my side cheering me through them. Destin is my biggest fan and cheerleader. With her by my side We May Not Have It All Together But Together We Have It All! Oh…. and if I forget to tell her, I HAD A GREAT TIME!

Book Description

In "My Raw Reality: From "Losing My Mind • Gaining My Faith," I invite you on an intimate journey of spiritual awakening and personal transformation. Through my narrative, I reveal how God directly intervened in My life, teaching Me profound truths that spiritual leaders never taught me.

I candidly explore the challenges of spiritual warfare and the hidden forces that can lead us astray. With unwavering honesty, I share my own struggle with depression and anxiety, and how, through divine guidance, I discovered my true identity as a beloved child of God. By stepping out of a victim mentality, I embrace my role as a victorious conqueror.

This book illuminates the complexities of emotional entanglements and soul ties, offering insight into how

God can break those chains. I shed light on the confusion often caused by religious institutions, revealing how I personally overcame feelings of unworthiness to embrace the unconditional love and acceptance of God.

Through my journey, I learned the transformative power of forgiveness, enabling myself to cultivate genuine friendships and establish peaceful relationships. I address my past, sharing raw and real experiences that some may find challenging. Yet, I believe that authenticity is crucial in a world weary of pretense.

With a heart full of love for Jesus, my mission is to set the record straight about His true nature, countering the misrepresentations that often arise in religious discourse. "Losing My Mind • Gaining My Faith" is not just a memoir; it is a beacon of hope for anyone seeking to break free from the chains of their past and embrace the faith that can lead to true freedom.

Join Me on this transformative journey, and discover how my own raw reality of Losing My Mind • Gaining My Faith can inspire you to reclaim your faith and live a life of purpose and victory

Into the Abyss

Brokenness from my divorce started my journey.

With divorce papers in hand, I was now a 30-year-old single mom of two boys. The weight of those papers felt heavier than a hundred-pound anchor, dragging me down to the depths of despair. But strangely, there was also a flicker of liberation. As soon as the ink dried, that defiant, crazy wild child—long stifled by the roles of wife and soccer mom—was unleashed into a world that had long forgotten her name.

From that moment on, I hit the clubs of Atlanta with reckless abandon. Night after night, I immersed myself in a whirlwind of partying and drinking, leaving my children in the care of babysitters while I chased the thrill I had deprived myself of for so long. Dancing under strobe lights, I became a fixture in the Atlanta nightlife scene, reveling in the attention that came with my new lifestyle. I was no longer just a mother; I was becoming part of the city's social fabric, a local celebrity in my own right. The thought of my boys left behind rarely crossed my mind with guilt. I was too caught up in the intoxicating whirlwind of nightlife and validation.

Surely, many of you can relate to the frantic search for sanity after enduring an excruciating divorce, especially when it's from the person you believed would be your forever. I was heartbroken and desperately seeking solace in any form I could find. It was during this chaotic time that I stumbled into the world of social media, a realm I had never known before. The attention from men was intoxicating; their compliments and flirtations were like sweet nectar for my wounded soul. I met a parade of beautiful faces, each one promising a distraction from my heartache.

Looking back, I chuckle at my naivety. So many of those "beautiful" men were likely nothing more than slimy perverts hiding behind flattering photos. I had stepped into a world I had no experience navigating, and I was utterly unprepared for what lay ahead.

Then, as if the Enemy of my soul was conspiring to lead me further down this reckless path, I met him—the "man of my dreams." His pictures displayed a man straight out of a fantasy, a real-life Prince Charming. With his piercing blue eyes and a façade that screamed success, he captivated me. He was older, seemingly well-established, and his social media was adorned with photos from glamorous photo shoots and magazine covers. I was a housewife turned party girl, suddenly dating an international male model. How surreal was that?

    Prince Charming was everything I needed to distract me from the pain of my past. He sent me daring emails filled with inappropriate pictures, something I had never encountered before. It thrilled me. I was addicted to the rush of being pursued in such a bold manner. The good girl in me was slowly fading, replaced by a woman eager to embrace risk and adventure. I found myself staying home more often, but only to indulge in late-night chats with him, neglecting my children in the process. I was entranced, unaware of how deeply I was being drawn into a web that would eventually ensnare me.

    Finally, after weeks of virtual romance, he invited me to meet him at an upscale restaurant. I was a bundle of nerves leading up to that night, my mind racing with anticipation. To calm myself, I indulged in a few drinks while getting ready—a decision that would prove disastrous. I had always prided myself on being responsible, but in that moment, I let my desire for excitement take the wheel.

Upon entering the restaurant, I spotted him instantly. He was even more handsome in person, and my heart raced as I took my seat across from him. He ordered me another glass of wine, and I drank it down eagerly, drowning my nerves in alcohol. But when I needed to use the restroom, things took an unexpected turn. He followed me, and in a moment of sheer audacity, he pushed me against the wall for a kiss. Mortified, I pushed him away, but a part of me was thrilled by the encounter. It was exhilarating and terrifying all at once.

As our relationship progressed, I found myself swept further into a world of recklessness. The more time we spent together, the crazier things became. I was entranced, like a moth drawn to a flame, willing to ignore the consequences of my actions. When he landed a job publishing a national magazine, complete with his own office in Atlanta, I felt like I had hit the jackpot. Here I was, dating a stunning man who was not only an international model but also the publisher of a national fashion magazine. My life had transformed in ways I had only dreamed of, and I was on top of the world—at least for the moment.

But beneath the surface, the fantasy was beginning to unravel. I had no idea how much I needed God, how desperately I would come to rely on the strength only He could provide. Little did I know, the journey ahead would lead me through darkness I could never have imagined, challenging everything I thought I knew about love, life, and myself.

Chapter One
The Unraveling of Legalism

In my journey through life, I often found myself ensnared in a web of expectations woven by those who claimed to know God best. They were the "Christians" who stood rigidly behind their doctrines, armed with rules and regulations that felt more like chains than guidance. Their words, laced with legalism, echoed in my mind, filling me with feelings of defeat and unworthiness. I was constantly reminded of my shortcomings, my struggles with dyslexia and ADHD adding layers of complexity to my already tumultuous relationship with faith. Reading the Bible was an arduous task; the long names and dense passages often left me frustrated and disheartened.

In Sunday school, I was taught that God's love hinged on performance—a conditional love that seemed to evaporate with each mistake I made. I remember sitting in the pews, feeling the weight of judgment pressing down on me. The very people who were meant to be vessels of grace instead became barriers to understanding God's true nature. I felt like an outsider, a spectator in a world where perfection was the standard, and I was anything but perfect.

Yet, in my deepest pain, God began to dismantle the falsehoods that had been built around my understanding of Him. It was during those darkest hours—when I felt most alone—that I sensed His presence most profoundly. God was not mad at me; He was not waiting to strike me down for my failings. Instead, He reached out to me as a friend, inviting me into a relationship that transcended the rigid confines of religious expectation.

It was in the stillness of those moments that I began to learn who God really is. He was not the distant deity I had imagined, but a loving Father who understood my struggles and met me where I was. Through prayer, not scripture, I found my voice. I poured out my heart to Him, sharing my fears and frustrations, and in return, I received comfort and clarity. God began to teach me lessons that I had never encountered in church; lessons not about condemnation, but about love and grace.

He showed me that the root of my struggles lay not in my actions, but in my heart. I realized that spiritual warfare wasn't just about fighting external battles, but also about confronting the lies I had internalized. I learned that God does not change us through guilt or shame; instead, He offers us an invitation to be transformed through His love. This revelation was liberating. I no longer needed to strive for perfection or hide behind a facade of righteousness. I could be real, honest, and raw with God.

As I grew in this understanding, my perspective shifted dramatically. I began to see the world not as a battleground of judgment, but as a canvas for love and grace. The people who once made me feel unworthy were transformed in my eyes. I saw their struggles, their fears, and their own battles with self-worth. I realized that we are all in this together, navigating our paths with varying degrees of success and failure.

I embraced my imperfections, knowing that they did not disqualify me from being loved by God. In fact, they equipped me to love others more deeply. I learned that my role as a believer was not to police others' behaviors but to walk alongside them in their journeys, offering support, prayer, and love. This was the essence of Christ's message, one that had been obscured by the legalism I had encountered.

God's grace became the foundation of my life. It was not about adhering to a set of rules but about cultivating a real relationship with Him—a relationship built on trust, love, and understanding. I could cuss, drink a little, and still be a follower of Christ, because my faith was not contingent upon my actions but rooted in God's unwavering love for me.

This chapter of my life is a testament to the transformative power of God's relationship. It is a reminder that we do not have to be perfect to be worthy of His love. In the unlikeliest of places, amidst the chaos of misunderstanding and judgment, I discovered freedom. Freedom to be myself, to embrace my journey, and to share that journey with others. God is not looking for polished performances; He desires authentic connections.

As I pen these words, I hope to illuminate the path for others who, like me, have felt the sting of legalism and the weight of unworthiness. I want to remind you that God's love is not contingent on your perfection but is a constant, unwavering presence in your life. You are worthy, you are loved, and you are not alone in this battle. Together, let us navigate the complexities of faith, stripping away the layers of misunderstanding to reveal the heart of God—a heart that loves us back to life.

Chapter Two
The Cycle of Insanity

The enemy sneaks into our lives, subtly breaking us down, piece by piece.

It wasn't long before I found myself caught in an eight-year cycle of insanity, a seemingly endless loop that I couldn't escape. Fast forward: Prince Charming, the man who had swept me off my feet, was hiding secrets beneath his beautiful façade—strongholds I was completely unaware of. So mesmerized by his allure and desperate to escape the pain of my divorce, I ignored the red flags and logical warning signs flashing before me like neon lights.

But I had my own issues from childhood that I had long suppressed, now resurfacing with a vengeance. The moment I fell in love and moved in with him, it became clear that the fairy tale was a façade. Prince Charming was beautiful, yes, but he also had a secret life. My heart shattered time and again as I uncovered the truth: he had hundreds of online girlfriends, some of whom he saw during working hours at his office. A male model/actor turned magazine publisher, he was constantly surrounded by stunning women. It never occurred to me what kind of lifestyle that entailed, and each new revelation felt like a dagger to my heart.

    The cycle of insanity began with my first breakup after nearly a year of tolerating his sex addiction and infidelity. When I finally gathered the courage to leave, he was gone for two weeks before pleading for me to take him back. In my state of raw pain, I relented, convinced he had changed, that he would never betray me again. How wrong I was.

    Over the next eight years, this cycle repeated itself with maddening regularity. They say insanity is doing the same thing over and over while expecting different results. This was my twisted cycle of insanity. Prince Charming continued to engage in sexual relationships with other women, arguing that he wasn't cheating because I never caught him in the act. Instead, I was forced to witness his provocative, sexually explicit online interactions. Each time he stayed out all night, he would belittle my feelings, insisting I was irrational and overreacting. He made me feel as though I were the crazy one for suspecting him, turning me into a paranoid lunatic who stayed up late, playing investigator in a desperate attempt to uncover the truth.

The pattern continued: we would break up, only to reconcile, and then the cycle would repeat. Each time we got back together, I felt as though I was losing my sanity. His apologies seemed sincere, and when he was caught, he acted as if I were the one in the wrong. He manipulated me into believing that my insecurities were pushing him away, only to run to another woman and then return, begging for forgiveness when he missed me. It took years for me to realize that I was addicted to him, obsessed to the point where I thought I couldn't live without him. Yet, in reality, there was never a moment in those eight years when I felt relaxed or secure. I was like a mother, perpetually spying on her troubled child, desperately trying to catch him in the act of wrongdoing. What was I thinking? I was thinking what so many others have thought: that love could change him, that my unwavering devotion would transform him into the man I wanted him to be.

Instead, I became the sad, insecure victim I never wanted to be. We changed each other, pushing one another further from anything godly. My life became a series of struggles, each one more overwhelming than the last. Just as I began to piece my life back together, I would lose everything again, all because of my obsession with this man. I was fixated on changing him, determined to make him see the depth of his issues. I found myself fighting for his heart, a battle I was all too familiar with. In my younger years, I had survived living in my car, scraping together food and a life. But this was different; this was a fight against something that had taken hold of my heart. I was worshiping a man as if he were my idol, playing God in a futile attempt to change him.

When he wasn't with me, my thoughts spiraled into darkness. I was tormented by the idea of him giving his heart to another woman. What if she made him fall in love with her? What if she made him become the version of him I had fought so hard to create? What if she was more beautiful? What if her body was perfect? I was consumed by desperation and heartache, trapped in a cycle of defeat and guilt.

I was doing everything the enemy wanted me to do—everything Satan hoped would throw me off track. He was determined to turn my life upside down, to keep me from stepping into my calling. The enemy knew exactly what I wanted and used that knowledge to try and destroy me. I'm certain that Prince Charming had no idea he was being used as a pawn in this twisted game. He was a wonderful man at heart, but his identity had been stolen by the enemy, just as mine had. We were both caught in destructive patterns we never intended to be a part of, oblivious to the fact that our behaviors would eventually lead to our own destruction if we didn't change.

    The enemy sneaks into our lives and slowly begins to break us down, bit by bit. My journey was a testament to the fragile nature of love, how easily our hearts and souls can get intertwined with someone and a soul bond can be created. I was witnessing how easily my heart and mind could be manipulated into something dark and twisted. And in that chaos, I was finally forced to confront the truth: I needed to break free from this cycle before it consumed me entirely. I just had no clue how to make things better or turn my seemingly twisted life and situations back around.

Chapter Three

From Darkness to Redemption

The Enemy's plot led to my depression, but God redeemed me.

In the depths of my despair, I found myself spiraling into a deep depression. For weeks, my broken heart kept me bound to my bed, paralyzed by feelings of hopelessness. Suicidal thoughts haunted me, a constant whisper of despair that echoed in my mind. I cried nonstop, consumed by grief and regret. But then, one day, everything shifted. God spoke to my heart, initiating a profound process of understanding and redemption.

He brought to mind the stories of biblical heroes—Christ, Moses, Noah, and others—reminding me how the enemy had tried to destroy them from childhood. The enemy sought to thwart their destinies, ensuring that these great leaders never fulfilled their God-given callings. He wanted to stop them before they could heal hearts, change lives, break free from bondage, and lead others to know their Heavenly Father.

In my own life, I realized that I too was being tempted by evil, lured into a toxic downward spiral designed to keep me from conquering adversity. But God reminded me of my strength, of my identity as His daughter, and of the source of my healing. He made it clear that to be free from the bondage I had endured since childhood, I needed to take steps I had never taken before.

The days of defiance and rebellion had begun long ago, rooted in the struggles of my youth. I thought I had outgrown them, but in reality, they had merely been suppressed, waiting for the right moment to resurface. As I faced my brokenness, I discovered strongholds that had been awakened by my pain. God explained that stepping out of these patterns would not be easy; it might even feel uncomfortable at times. But I was ready for real change. I was fed up with the pain and confusion, so I made the decision to walk with Him.

I had always known God and identified as a Christian, but I had never truly walked with Him until I surrendered everything on that pivotal day. From that moment forward, I began my journey, committing myself to walk with God wholeheartedly.

The first thing I did after turning my life over to Jesus was to reconnect with my children. I realized how much I had missed being the mom they deserved. They were, without a doubt, the most important parts of my life. The enemy tried to plant feelings of guilt in my mind, reminding me of the times I had neglected their needs for a man. But those thoughts didn't linger long. God reminded me that I had been in pain, confused and broken, and that I hadn't been thinking clearly. I repented and chose to move forward.

I understood that I needed to distance myself from anyone or anything that held me back from moving on. I knew it wouldn't be easy, but I was finally ready. During this transformative period, I confronted issues I had long ignored—things that hindered my walk with God. He revealed to me, piece by piece, everything I needed to do to step into my calling and reach my destiny.

God instructed me to break ungodly soul ties and yokes that had shackled me for years. He helped me understand why I consistently attracted the same kinds of people and why I often found myself playing the "victim" role. He showed me aspects of myself that I needed to change—spiritually ugly things that had been hidden for too long.

I learned that prayer was more than just speaking to Him and walking away. I had to sit still and listen to His voice. God loved that I talked to Him, but He wanted me to hear Him in return. He had so much to tell me, yet in the past, I had never paused long enough to listen. No one had ever taught me the importance of that part of prayer. So, I began to pray and listen. In my quiet moments, I painted canvases that took days to finish, using that time to talk to Him and hear from Him. It became my special time with God.

Before I embarked on this journey, I had dismissed the notion of "hearing from God" as nonsense. I was the last person to raise my hands in church, cry during praise and worship, or engage in a genuine conversation with God. But as I began to speak to Him like a friend and truly listened, He spoke so clearly and profoundly to me. His words resonated in a way I could understand.

God provided signs and confirmations that it was indeed Him speaking to me. He would prompt me to look up a devotional I had never read before, and when I did, I was amazed to find it addressed the very things He was placing on my heart. I would turn on the TV to find a pastor delivering a message that perfectly aligned with what God was teaching me. These seemingly random occurrences happened so frequently that I often felt I was in a surreal twilight zone.

He would give me specific numbers to write down. Hours later, I would glance at a clock or my phone, only to see those same numbers. I would randomly open my Bible to the exact page or verse that corresponded to those numbers. Then, I began having dreams and visions that came to fruition. One miraculous event after another unfolded, confirming that my relationship with God was growing deeper.

The closer I drew to God, the more His presence became palpable in my life.

John 16:33 reminds us, "I have told you these things, so that in me you may have peace. In this world, you will have trouble. But take heart! I have overcome the world." I held onto that promise as I stepped into my new life, knowing that with God, I was finally on the path to healing and redemption. The darkness that once threatened to consume me was receding, replaced by a light that filled my heart with hope and purpose.

Chapter Four
The Teacher of My Heart

When God started teaching me, everything changed.

I grew up with severe dyslexia and ADD, struggles that shaped my childhood and influenced my self-perception. I had never read a book until I was in my 30s, and the enemy reveled in that fact. He sat back, laughing, knowing that the labels of dyslexia and ADD would become the very identity I carried. Satan was corrupting the identity God had given me, twisting it into something that made me feel insecure and unworthy.

Looking back now, I can't help but laugh. While I was in learning disability (LD) classes, feeling abnormal, I was also voted into favorites and homecoming court by students in regular classes. God ensured the enemy didn't steal too much of my confidence. He counteracts everything the enemy tries to do to destroy us, and I was beginning to see that truth unfold in my life.

As my relationship with God deepened, He reminded me that all those years I felt inferior and less intelligent, it was merely the enemy planting lies in my head to throw me off track. I was worthy, and I had a significant purpose. The enemy knew this and would stop at nothing to try to destroy it before I realized what I was capable of achieving.

Up until that point, I could never focus long enough to read the Bible or understand any part of it. To me, it was a jumbled mess. The long, complex names—like "Nebuchadnezzar"—only added to my confusion. By the time I managed to pronounce a name, I had forgotten what the passage was about. God knew all of this about me. He made me, and He was there every time the enemy whispered lies into my mind, trying to make me feel defeated.

But God didn't lay blame or conviction on me; instead, He loved me back to restoration. He gently guided me through each obstacle, one by one. There was no rush, no pressure to feel unworthy of His love. One day, while cleaning the bookshelf, my son's children's Bible fell out. As I opened it, everything changed. The words were simpler, and the pages were filled with vibrant, colorful pictures. This was God's way of leading me to start reading the Bible.

He then encouraged me to play a game: "Open up to anywhere in the Bible and see what it says." Each time I did, the verses spoke directly to my heart, offering the comfort and guidance I desperately needed. Before this revelation, I had attended churches where I felt like an outcast, surrounded by people who could recite scriptures effortlessly. I felt inadequate, believing that maybe I wasn't as close to God as I thought—perhaps I wasn't even worthy.

The enemy had used other Christians to make me feel defeated and unworthy, particularly because I was different. But God, the coolest teacher ever, started instructing me in ways that only I could understand. He revealed truths that resonated deeply within me, and I became passionate about learning more about Him and His Word. Growing up, I had thought that reading and understanding the Bible was the most crucial aspect of being a Christian. You can imagine my frustration when I felt close to God, yet struggled to comprehend His Word.

Then God began to speak to me in ways that made sense. He reminded me who inspired the authors of the Bible—the same God who spoke to them would guide me. He explained that many people today have things out of order and teach incorrectly, leaving new Christians bewildered. While His words in the Bible are vital, the most important part of being a Christian is the relationship between His children and Himself.

He reassured me that once I learned how to talk to Him and listen to what He had to say, everything else would begin to fall into place on my journey. He told me that if He could give the authors of the Bible the words to write, He could also speak to me through our conversations. He wanted me to know that I could look up what He told me in the Scriptures for confirmation that it was truly from Him.

In those moments, He showed me that my discouragement was blocking valuable time I could have spent with Him. I realized that I was not only capable of understanding His Word but that He was actively guiding me through this new and exciting journey of faith.

As I embraced this new perspective, Scripture began to resonate deeply within me. Philippians 4:13 echoed in my heart: "I can do all things through Him who strengthens me." Deuteronomy 31:8 became a comforting reminder: "The LORD himself goes before you and will be with you; he will never leave you nor forsake you. Do not be afraid; do not be discouraged." I clung to the truth in 1 Peter 4:13: "But rejoice in as much as you participate in the sufferings of Christ, so that you may be overjoyed when his glory is revealed." And Isaiah 41:13 reassured me: "For I am the LORD your God who takes hold of your right hand and says to you, Do not fear; I will help you."

With each passing day, I learned to embrace my identity as a child of God, free from the lies of the enemy. God was teaching me to read not just the words on the page but the truths of who He is and who I was created to be. My journey was just beginning, but now, I was walking hand in hand with my Creator, ready to discover the incredible plans He had for my life.

Chapter Five
The Depths of Understanding

The reality is that God is so much more than what I had ever been taught.

As my relationship with Him deepened, God began to speak to my heart about my sins in a way that was both gentle and revealing. Throughout my life, church communities often made me feel as though sin was a sign that I wasn't truly a Christian. But God reminded me of His Word, specifically the verse that says, "He who is without sin cast the first stone." He emphasized that we all face different circumstances and battles. He asked me, "How are you going to overcome those battles with victory if you don't walk this journey with me and allow me to crush each adversity one by one? How would you learn anything from those battles if you instantly found yourself in a perfect place?"

God made it clear that He understood no one would navigate life flawlessly, adhering to every commandment. Jesus was the only man free from sin. We are all sinners, and He gave us commandments not as a means of condemnation but as something to refer to when we are struggling in life. When we feel as though everything seems to be causing us pain and difficulty. That's when I had my Ah Ha! moment and realized commandments were simply a navigation tool designed to help us understand what we were doing wrong. To fix a problem, you must recognize its root of where the problem came from.

God taught me that while many with a "religious spirit" admonish others to stop sinning and follow the commandments to avoid hell, they often neglect the critical step of addressing the root of the problem first. Many preach about the dangers of sin without discussing spiritual warfare, the reasons we sin, or how to stop. The very people that seemed to make me feel unworthy, were also dealing with their own struggles and brokenness. I realized that some needed to point out my shortcomings in order to make themselves feel like a better person.

It also occurred to me that without God preparing another's heart and mind, he will not instruct you to tell them anything about their faults. He would never instruct anyone to go to a broken person to change their mind about sinning unless he already prepared them to hear and listen.

Not everyone is your assignment. I believe that you should never make people feel unworthy. And if you are concerned about them doing wrong things, you should never discuss their sins without them knowing your heart and feeling comfortable enough with you to receive what advice or lecture you have for them. Also, my belief is that God would give you wisdom to explain to them how to pray effectively to combat the enemy.

God revealed to me the concept of generational behaviors and soul ties. He explained that each time we break a commandment, we inadvertently grant the enemy and demonic influences of authority to invade our lives and wreak havoc. Unfortunately, throughout my life, I had attended many churches that never taught me about these realities. I had no idea that what the Bible referred to as being "knit together" was a soul tie, or that a yoke was a spiritual burden. I always assumed it was something in an egg. Perhaps more pastors should delve into these profound topics instead of merely preaching and reading scripture. When explained properly, these concepts and truths are not only interesting but crucial to understanding our faith. Also crucial to break strongholds, generational curses and ungodly soul ties.

I pondered how Jesus loved everyone so profoundly when He walked the earth. He didn't merely recite God's Word; He explained it in ways that were accessible and relatable. He addressed the spiritual issues within us, yet somehow, I had never been taught this during my years in church. Why didn't they explain things as Jesus did? Did they fully understand these truths themselves? Why were so many quick to condemn me to hell for my sins? Why did leaders and other followers of Christ make me feel the need to be perfect before I could draw close to Jesus? Why did so many make me think it was wrong to be transparent about what my shortcomings were and how bad I was in my past.

I was always transparent but these religious people made me feel ashamed. Why was there such a lack of teaching on how to recognize and combat the demonic influences that were at play in my life? Some of the issues I was dealing with were even caused after humans misled and abused me when they always talked like they knew Jesus. Why was it not known that in order to fix issues or strongholds, we have to be honest about what is going on or what we went through so others know what to pray for? I had so many questions.

I had never realized that simply being around people who engaged in evil activities and participating in those behaviors myself could grant authority to demonic forces over my life. There was so much more depth to all of this than I had been led to believe. Some viewed God as merely a man who labeled Himself God and penned nonsensical rules in a book. On the other end of the spectrum were the "religious people" who wielded the Bible to elevate their own status above others.

But the reality is that God is so much more than that. The things of God are profound and intricate, meant to bring us comfort, wisdom and understanding rather than shame or despair.

Finally, I began to grasp why He established the commandments. It wasn't to control or condemn us; it was rooted in His immense love, designed to keep us safe. I believe many people, like me, would willingly obey the commandments if they truly understood their purpose and the consequences of breaking them.

God revealed to me the importance of each commandment and how we, as humans, had often misinterpreted them, leading to confusion. For example, when you read to not use God's name in vain I had always thought it referred solely to cursing or using His name disrespectfully. While that does offend some and doing things we know offend certain people is wrong, the deeper meaning is about using God's name to gain respect or mislead others. Many manipulate their authority in the church for selfish gain, utilizing God as a tool to exploit others.

Another commandment that is often misunderstood is to "love thy neighbor as thyself." Many struggle to love themselves, which makes it difficult to love others. Some might even narrow this commandment down to simply loving the neighbor next door, which can be challenging if they throw loud parties or let their dog poop on your lawn. But the truth is that loving your neighbor encompasses loving everyone—an enormous challenge indeed!

God desires to help us see our true identities and teaches us how to love ourselves so that we can extend that love to others. He wants us to first know Him as a friend and Heavenly Father before he expects us to focus on being "perfect" and repenting for our shortcomings.

One more commandment that may seem obvious but carries profound meaning is the commandment against killing. While we understand that this refers to physical killing out of anger, rage or perversion, if you open your spiritual eyes and dig deeper, scripture reveals that the enemy seeks to kill, steal, and destroy. Killing can refer not only to physical violence but also to the destruction of dreams, childhood innocence, and future potential. The enemy aims to ruin relationships, homes, lives and more.

The word "kill" in that commandment represents more than I had ever imagined. While I don't want to delve too deeply into the commandments, I hope you grasp the essence of what I'm saying and what I believe to be true.

Jeremiah 1:5 reminds us, "Before I formed you in the womb, I knew you; before you were born, I set you apart." God knows us intimately and has a plan for each of us, and in that knowledge, we can find comfort and strength as we navigate our journeys with Him. Understanding the depth of His love and the purpose behind His commandments has transformed my relationship with God, turning fear into trust and confusion into clarity. With trust, I'm also understanding that submitting to him is a natural reaction.

Chapter Six

Sharpening Each Other's Swords

After so many days of fasting and praying I heard God speaking to my heart saying that the most important thing to Him is our relationship.

After years of struggle and searching, I finally gained wisdom and was ready for the next part of my journey. My interest in spiritual warfare began to blossom, and I felt a tug on my heart to explore this new territory. God delighted in the way I spoke to Him, just as I would with my best friend. He revealed to me that the enemy works hard to block communication between God and His children. The enemy fosters feelings of unworthiness when we stumble and fail, making us believe we don't know the "right" way to pray. This sense of defeat can stop us from praying altogether.

But God reassured me: if you don't understand or read the Bible yet, if you still sin or aren't sure how to pray, He will help you with all of it. He wants us to start talking to Him as if He were our best friend. He longs for all of us to hear what He has to say in return so that He can teach us. When we allow Him to lead us, everything begins to fall into place. He will transform our mind, making His desires our own.

One day, you may find that you haven't had a drink or a cigarette in weeks. Perhaps your desire to sleep around with random people will fade, maybe you don't feel like hanging out at the clubs to party like you once did. You may suddenly realize you haven't thought about the temptations that once held you captive. God doesn't expect us to navigate this journey on our own. He understands the enemy's tactics—how we get tricked and tempted. God will guide you in understanding and following His commandments once you start walking with Him and trusting Him. Even then we will always be learning.

As I continued to seek God, He spoke to me about writing this book. He assured me that many others have been held back from experiencing total freedom and a beautiful relationship with Him. They simply do not understand. He wanted me to share what He had shown me so that others could have their own "Ah Ha" moments, just like I had. God has a way of turning the most painful experiences into something beautiful. He took my broken heart and insecurities—those very things meant to discourage and stop me—and transformed them into my testimony.

Little did I know that the enemy's attempt to use Prince Charming to break me would ultimately lead me to reach out and start my walk with God. The battle was not one-sided; Satan was also trying to kill Prince Charming's spirit through me. Listening to God opened my eyes to my own faults in the relationship. I learned how to accept responsibility for my actions. Acknowledging my shortcomings helped me heal so many injured parts of myself and transform, preventing me from falling back into old patterns. It made me realize that I could no longer blame my poor decisions on others, nor could I continue to view myself as a victim.

Just because many churches don't explain spiritual warfare doesn't mean you shouldn't attend. You will always be learning. One of the wisest humans I ever met once told me to "chew up the meat and spit out the bones" meaning go somewhere you feel led and comfortable. Congregate and listen to the pastor. If there is something that you aren't feeling led to retain and use mentally, then discard it from your thoughts and carry on.

There are wonderful blessings that come from finding a good church home. I went through a season of loneliness, and my church family became my sheltering trees. They were always willing to stop and pray with me when I needed support. I encourage you to get plugged into a church with a solid biblical foundation and who hear the Holy Spirit and not their flesh. Sometimes they even become as close as family.

Once you understand how to start this journey and trust God to take care of everything along the way, you open the door to total freedom. You may one day help others understand their own journeys. Lives could be transformed as you become a vessel for God's work. Who knows? Maybe church leaders will learn from you.

Each chapter of this book was written to share my experiences and includes instructions from God that helped me navigate adversity. I know many of you will relate because Satan is generic in how he attacks; he employs the same tactics against us all. The good news is that we can learn from one another. We can teach each other strategies to fight back and win each battle.

We sharpen one another's swords.

Hebrews 4:12 tells us, "For the word of God is quick, and powerful, and sharper than any two-edged sword, piercing even to the dividing asunder of soul and spirit, and of the joints and marrow, and is a discerner of the thoughts and intents of the heart." This verse serves as a reminder of the strength and power of God's Word in our lives. As we walk this journey together, let us encourage and uplift one another, sharpening our swords in the process, so that we can stand strong against the enemy and boldly pursue the beautiful relationship God desires for each of us.

Chapter Seven
No One Is Immune

Do you remember the joy of playing in your mom's makeup, feeling grown-up and pretty? Or sitting in your mom or dad's lap, pretending to steer the car, and imagining yourself behind the wheel? How about the thrill of climbing the tallest tree, reaching the top to take in the view, and feeling a mix of excitement and nervousness as the wind made the branches sway? When you finally descended, you could brag about your adventure!

What about the delight of choosing the pants and shoes you wanted, just to fit in with your peers? The excitement of getting a trendy haircut that made you feel like you belonged? Do you recall the first time your mom let you get highlights or when she finally agreed to pierce your ears? Those moments were truly magical, weren't they?

Now, imagine if you could retrain your mind to reconnect with that childlike spirit. Where all of the things we got excited about were so authentic and innocent. Nobody cared about your financial status or what color you were. Where you didn't feel less than if you couldn't fit in with the trends because nobody really cared but it was fun to match what others had. This was back when you were very young of course.

Then things started evolving and insecurity sat in. Not with just you but with those around you. That insecurity caused others and maybe even yourself to project hatred and bullying. Then you started to feel obligated to wear or do what others did. It almost became a chore and you worried what others would think and say if you didn't follow and strive to be like the one everyone followed.

What if you could embrace the truth that you are already beautiful, amazing, and absolutely fantastic just as you are—without all the superficial things we feel we need to gain acceptance? What if, as you delve deeper into your spiritual self and discover who you were truly meant to be, you realize that all those years spent striving for perfection to earn love and acceptance were unnecessary?

I am a former national platform artist, salon owner, hair stylist, makeup artist, and photographer. I built my career on making people look and feel beautiful, ensuring they left the salon with evidence of their beauty—a stunning, edited photo to showcase on social media. This way, they had proof of a day when they felt confident and radiant. People would tell my clients how gorgeous they were, and they needed that validation to believe in their own beauty and style. I did this for both women and men (though no makeup for men), fully aware of the need for validation that often stems from lies told to us by the enemy.

Why did I understand this need so well? Because as a pre teen I never felt beautiful when I looked in the mirror. I battled with body dysmorphic disorder from the time I was old enough to form an identity of my own. I didn't realize back then that the enemy was the source of my insecurity; I simply thought that no matter how many compliments I received, people were lying to me. I would stare at my reflection as a very skinny preteen and cry, convinced I was a chubby girl. I scrutinized my face, feeling deformed and disproportionate. I could see my bones poking out in some places while fat accumulated in others, and I felt gross.

Reflecting on my childhood, I remembered being told daily that I was "good for nothing" by my stepfather.

I listened to him call my mother a "stupid fat b**ch" throughout my formative years (and she wasn't even overweight). Many of you reading this can understand the damage such words can inflict on a child. As a kid, I thought it was normal. I was so unhappy but didn't know any better; I accepted my life as it was. My stepmother at that time introduced me to smoking, drinking wine, and even playing with the Ouija board. For the record, my current stepmother of 35 plus years is not the woman I described above.

In that other household, my stepfather belittled everyone, often resorting to physical abuse against my brothers and me. Every other word out of his mouth was a demeaning cuss word. He yelled at us 90% of the time. I lived in constant fear, too afraid to speak up. I felt inadequate and unprotected. Even my mother was manipulated, used and abused.

Most weekends, I would lay on my bedroom floor, staring at the shapes in the carpet, crying and feeling utterly alone. I didn't go to movies or hang out at the mall often like most teenagers. My mother felt pressured to keep quiet, fearing that if she spoke out, we would be thrown into homelessness. For many years, I blamed her until I grew up and realized the pain she endured from the same abuse. As an adult, I learned how easy it is to say what you would and wouldn't tolerate until you face that reality yourself. My mom was a victim too. I later learned that as a child I had no control over being victimized but as an adult it was my responsibility to start my healing journey to ensure my brokenness didn't cause toxicity to be protected onto others.

Let me clarify: my parents were good people, and we have great relationships now. They had no idea of the extent of the abuse I was experiencing by both of their significant other. I know some of you are thinking that you wouldn't have allowed yourself to get so lost in your circumstances. I used to think that way too, until I truly began to heal. I came to understand that each one of us goes through experiences that others might shake their heads at or judge.

No one is immune.

The fact that you are reading this book tells me you're grappling with past and present hurts. The purpose of this book is to allow you to walk alongside me on my journey of finding the key to unlock the door to freedom. Broken chains and true self-love and acceptance can only be found through God. I struggled my entire life until I was faced with suicidal thoughts. At that moment, I realized something had to change. I wasn't going to let the enemy win. I had fought too hard to survive, and I wasn't about to give up.

Looking back at the most challenging moments of my life, I recognized that following through with suicide would mean giving up on that younger version of myself who fought so hard to get to where I was at that time. I would have been abandoning my purpose—the purpose God had designed for me. I refused to close the door on my own potential. Those painful experiences had shaped my character. Beneath the walls I'd built around my heart, behind my defensiveness and my street-smart demeanor, lay a warm, kind soul who loved people deeply and simply wanted to be loved in return. I was just so misunderstood.

Ephesians 1:5 reminds us, "He predestined us for adoption to sonship through Jesus Christ, in accordance with his pleasure and will." Romans 6:6 reassures us that "our old self was crucified with him so that the body ruled by sin might be done away with, that we should no longer be slaves to sin." And Romans 8:37 declares, "But in all these things we overwhelmingly conquer through Him who loved us."

The truth is, no one is immune to the struggles of life. But there is hope, healing, and transformation available to all of us. As I continue my journey, I invite you to join me in discovering the beauty of who you truly are, free from the lies that have held you captive for far too long. Together, we can walk toward freedom, love, and acceptance through the grace of God.

Chapter Eight
The Courageous Conqueror

    God desires for us to look forward, using our past as a stepping stone for progress rather than a source of pain. When I embarked on my transformative journey, God made it clear: I had to stop being a victim. You will see this theme throughout my story—speaking victory over our lives and circumstances is crucial. Yes, you may have been a victim at some point, but you cannot fully step into the role of a survivor until you recognize the courageous conqueror that resides within you—the person God created you to be.

    Each one of us is designed to be a survivor. God walks with us through the storms of our lives, equipping us with the sword to fight our battles. His encouragement comes not just from the scriptures but through personal revelations that strengthen our faith. He sharpens our swords and prepares us for the day when we will share our stories and help others. God never allows us to endure hardships without a purpose; He transforms our struggles into beautiful testimonies.

Reflecting on my own journey, I realize I would have never discovered my strength if God had simply removed all the challenges from my path. Instead, He became my teacher, granting me wisdom to overcome adversity. I grew proud—not only of my resilience but of my relationship with God.

I remember a particular moment a few years ago when I watched a video of a seemingly perfect couple. The boyfriend proposed to his beautiful girlfriend through a flash mob, dancing to "I Think I Want to Marry You." The sight of the tiny, gorgeous blonde, no more than 24 years old, leaping into his arms as he presented the ring left me feeling despondent. At that time, I was approaching 41, having experienced a marriage and divorce, several failed relationships, and the ongoing struggles of single parenting with three almost-grown children. I was overwhelmed with thoughts of regret, wondering, "If I had just gotten my life together at that age, perhaps I would be happily married with well-rounded children and a thriving career."

In that moment of despair, God spoke to my heart. He reminded me that I was successful and beautiful in my own right, having accomplished so much already. He told me to look beyond the façade of that video, which the enemy used to fill my mind with lies and negative thoughts. I was instructed to focus not on my past failures but on how far I had come.

God also revealed to me the patterns of generational behavior and soul ties that had been passed down through my family line. Issues such as allowing abuse, mental illness, physical illness (as a result of poor nutrition), eating disorders, addiction, etc… had created a cycle of pain that different family members struggled with. Some of the behaviors and addictions our ancestors struggled with were had unknowingly continued to pass on to our children. Understanding the roots of these behaviors took years of struggle, but it also illuminated why our bloodlines often repeated the same mistakes

True deliverance from these patterns can only come from God. This is why therapy and rehab often provide only temporary relief for many. God invites us to seek His guidance, encouraging not just prayer but also listening for His voice. He teaches us lessons the world cannot offer. When I began my journey with Him, He assured me that I was made new. By allowing Him to guide me, I became capable of achieving everything my heart desired—desires that would transform my life and future along the way.

Walking with Jesus shifted my perspective. He restored the life that the enemy had stolen from me, reclaiming my identity that had been distorted by years of hurt. Through this process, I learned that my worth was not tied to my appearance or how I could make others feel. I had been confused, believing that validation came from being pretty and also helping those who didn't deserve my time and energy. This confusion led me to share my light with counterfeit people leaving me so battered and broken mentally and so physically worn down.

But God intervened, revealing the truth. He cleaned me up and made me new again, showing me that even those who seem perfect or have fewer scars still have battles to fight. Everyone has their own journey, and their mistakes will come to light one day. For me, the focus needed to be on the beauty within myself. A beauty that only my Heavenly Father could create.

God wants us to look forward and only glance back to see progress, not pain. He is our shield and our glory, lifting our heads high. As I reflect on my transformation, I am reminded of the promises found in Scripture:

Psalm 3:3: "But you, LORD, are a shield around me, my glory, the One who lifts my head high."

2 Corinthians 1:3-4: "Praise be to the God and Father of our Lord Jesus Christ, the Father of compassion and the God of all comfort, who comforts us in all our troubles, so that we can comfort those in any trouble with the comfort we ourselves receive from God."

1 Peter 2:9: "But you are a chosen people, a royal priesthood, a holy nation, God's special possession, that you may declare the praises of him who called you out of darkness into his wonderful light."

As we navigate our journeys, let us remember to look forward with hope, to trust in the transformation that God is bringing forth, and to recognize the courageous conqueror within us.

Chapter Nine
The Master of Counterfeit

"Dear friends, do not be surprised at the fiery ordeal that has come on you to test you, as though something strange were happening to you." — 1 Peter 4:12

The enemy is a liar. He is the master of counterfeit, weaving deception into the very fabric of our lives. His goal is to distract us from our true identity and purpose, placing people in our paths who speak lies over us—lies that distort our self-perception and lead us to self-destruction. The enemy wants us weak, gradually tearing us down until we feel there is nothing worth living for. He thrives on our feelings of unworthiness, convincing us that no one will want us and that we will never be good enough. But that is a lie!

Remember this: the enemy knew the day we were conceived that we had a purpose. He has been working tirelessly ever since to silence us, to shut us down, and to stop us from fulfilling our God-given destiny.

Think back to your childhood. Some of us may have experienced a joyful upbringing, while others have endured hell on earth from an early age. Regardless of your past, I want to encourage you: God is turning that around. The years ahead are the years of divine reversal for you. God is making beauty from your ashes. He is taking every single thing the enemy tries to use to kill your spirit and is transforming those very struggles into stepping stones. What used to be your ceiling is now your floor.

No longer do we have to fill those empty spaces stolen from us in childhood with destructive habits or addictions. God will take away the negative and fill each crevice of our hearts with love, light, and truth. We can let go of the guilt for our past mistakes—God erases those too.

However, we must understand that sometimes we have to trust and believe we are redeemed before we can fully walk in that redemption. Jesus is the only one who can truly validate us, and He will remove any urge we have to seek fulfillment in anything other than Him. I can speak to this truth because I, too, have undergone this life-changing process. God opened my eyes to see things I had never seen before. He closed doors that needed to be shut and opened better ones—doors that no man or spirit can close. These are the doors meant for you, where your true identity will shine, revealing God's light to those around you.

When we identify ourselves by what the world says, we will always find ourselves striving to be good enough for others and even for ourselves. We become trapped in a cycle of seeking approval. But when we choose to walk with Jesus on this journey called life, we realize that His approval is all that matters. Jesus approved of you and me the moment we were conceived. He has called you beautiful, perfectly made, and worthy since before the day you took your first breath.

As we start to follow Christ, we stop trying to pick up on everyone else's personalities that seem appealing. Doesn't that sound like a relief? We can simply be ourselves because God designed us uniquely for a reason. We are more than enough just as we are, living our lives on purpose.

When you identify with Christ, you will begin to see yourself the way He sees you. And guess what? People will be drawn to that authentic version of you. The Christ within you will inspire others to seek the same connection. It is an attractive quality—comforting, refreshing, and transparent.

God made no one else like you for a reason. He crafted you with your quirks, flaws, and all, to walk the journey He has intended solely for you. Isn't that a beautiful thought? He has given each of us a unique style. People in this world may imitate, but they can never duplicate what God has created in you. So stop worrying about acceptance from others. Quit wishing for a different skin color, eye color, or the size your best friend wears. Don't envy their life, their job, or their spouse. The truth is, you wouldn't be as extraordinary as you are now if you had what they have. I'm speaking to myself also by saying these things because I too go backwards sometimes and struggle with my identity. I too sometimes still feel like I need to look a certain way for people to love and respect me. It's a constant battle but the battle is not ours while walking with Christ. He takes those burdens from us.

In order to effectively combat the adversary of our souls, it is crucial to recognize the various tactics he employs to distort our self-perception. Just as a general studies the patterns, strategies, and characteristics of an opponent to gain the upper hand in battle, we too must familiarize ourselves with the enemy's methods. By understanding these tactics, we can equip ourselves with the insights necessary to navigate our spiritual warfare more effectively.

The following list outlines several tactics that may resonate with your experiences, illustrating that you are not alone in facing these challenges. Remember, these struggles do not define your worth or qualifications; rather, they are manifestations of a supernatural evil force intent on frustrating and distracting you. This force seeks to implant negative thoughts in your mind, fostering feelings of inadequacy and discomfort in your own skin. When you succumb to these feelings, you may find yourself hesitating to embrace your true identity, which can hinder your growth and progress toward walking in freedom. Ultimately, this could lead to regression, preventing you from stepping fully into your God-given identity and realizing your full potential.

1. Lies and Deception: The enemy is identified as a liar who spreads falsehoods about our worth and identity. He uses deceit to make us believe that we are unworthy, not good enough, and that nobody will want us.

2. Counterfeit Relationships: The enemy places people in our lives who may contribute to our feelings of inadequacy or self-doubt. These relationships can lead us to self-destruct and adopt false narratives about ourselves.

3. Feelings of Unworthiness: The enemy thrives on making us feel unworthy, manipulating our emotions to the point where we believe we have nothing valuable to offer.

4. Comparison: This highlights the tendency to compare ourselves to others, leading to envy and discontent. This comparison can make us feel inadequate and diminish our sense of self-worth.

5. Seeking Approval from the World: When we identify ourselves based on societal standards or the opinions of others, we become trapped in a cycle of seeking external validation. This can further distort our self-perception and make us feel like we are never "good enough."

6. Past Experiences: The enemy can exploit past traumas or negative experiences to create a distorted self-image, convincing us that we are defined by those experiences rather than by our inherent worth as children of God.

7. Self-Destructive Behaviors: This is the tendency to fill emotional voids with addictions or harmful behaviors, which can stem from a distorted self-perception and lead to further degradation of self-worth.

Overall, these strategies work together to create a false identity that contrasts sharply with the truth of who we are as beloved creations of God. This encourages recognizing and rejecting these lies to embrace a true, God-given identity.

The enemy not only wants to steal your identity but also seeks to undermine those you admire. They may be wishing they were more like you, too! Wanting to be like someone else and being dissatisfied with who He made you to be is like saying that God makes errors. Remember, God makes no mistakes.

He is making beauty from your ashes.

"Before I formed you in the womb I knew you, before you were born I set you apart; I appointed you as a prophet to the nations!" — Jeremiah 1:5

"See what great love the Father has lavished on us, that we should be called children of God! And that is what we are! The reason the world does not know us is that it did not know him." — 1 John 3:1

"Dear friends, now we are children of God, and what we will be has not yet been made known. But we know that when Christ appears, we shall be like him, for we shall see him as he is." — 1 John 3:2

"But in all these things we overwhelmingly conquer through Him who loves us." — Romans 8:37

"So God created mankind in his own image, in the image of God he created them; male and female he created them." — Genesis 1:27

As we embrace our true identities in Christ, we can stand firm against the lies of the enemy. We are not defined by our past, nor by the voices that seek to diminish us. Instead, we are children of God, created for a purpose, and destined for greatness. Let us step boldly into the future, trusting in the beauty that God is creating from our ashes.

Chapter Ten
Filled with His Love — Your True Identity in Christ

In a world filled with competing narratives and self-doubt, it is essential to understand that you are who God says you are. He fills all the empty places within us with His love, and this truth forms the foundation of our identity in Christ. Unfortunately, many individuals miss out on this profound revelation because spiritual leaders sometimes focus on feelings of unworthiness rather than emphasizing the grace and love that God extends to each of us. It's all too common to encounter ego-driven "Christians" who, in an attempt to elevate their own sense of worth, point out the faults of others. This behavior stems from their inability to confront their own shortcomings.

When you stumble or make mistakes, the true essence of Christ within a genuine friend or leader will manifest as love and support. They will approach you with compassion, helping you recognize the issue and guiding you toward a solution. Christ's mission is about loving you back to life, cultivating a relationship built on friendship rather than exclusion. A true friend or spiritual leader who embodies the love of Jesus will celebrate your worthiness and accomplishments far more than any mistakes you may have made. The enemy, on the other hand, employs scare tactics and condemnation to keep you in a cycle of self-doubt and despair.

It is crucial to understand that your true identity can only be found in what Jesus says about you. You belong to God! You are part of the royal bloodline of the King of Kings, entitled to an inheritance rich with treasures both in heaven and on earth. If you have struggled with financial hardship, it's time to recognize that you are a prince or princess in God's kingdom. He has a divine inheritance planned for you, one that liberates you from the chains of poverty and lack. No son or daughter of God is destined to live in scarcity.

Moreover, if you have battled with any disorder or addiction, know that you are still His beloved child. God fills all the empty spaces in your life with His unwavering love and assurance, and you do not need to seek validation from the lies of the enemy any longer. God has a beautiful plan for each of His sons and daughters, a plan that instills confidence in your value and the value of everyone and everything you encounter.

When you embrace your identity as a child of God, you gain clarity about who is for you and who is against you. You will develop an awareness of those who genuinely appreciate your gifts and those who may seek to exploit them. In a world that often judges based on appearances or actions, you will find the boldness to stand firm in your identity in Christ. The opinions of others will no longer have the power to sway you.

The next time someone speaks unkindly about you, remember these five powerful words: "I don't identify with that." This simple declaration can serve as a shield against the arrows of negativity, allowing you to remain anchored in your identity.

God will also bless you with friendships that are truly treasures. These are people who will respect your relationships, uplift you, and stand by you, rather than betray or belittle you. They will not engage in gossip or manipulation; instead, they will celebrate your accomplishments even when you are not present. God will introduce you to individuals who recognize your value and provide opportunities for growth.

In terms of romantic relationships, God will guide you toward a love that is authentic and patient. This right person will appreciate you for who you are—whether you are at your heaviest or your lightest, whether you are wealthy or facing challenges. They will notice the unique qualities about you that others may have overlooked. God will teach you the essence of true love, and you may need to cultivate patience as you embrace this new experience.

For those already married, it's critical to understand that God can intervene in your situation. If your marriage was not ordained by Him and if both parties are unwilling to work on the relationship, God may lead you to a necessary release. However, He is also capable of transforming your spouse for the better. While I may not know the specifics of your circumstances, I do know that if you surrender everything to God, trust Him, and remain faithful, He will change your situation and restore the person He created you to be.

Understanding our identity in Christ is important for several key reasons:

1. Foundation of Self-Worth: Recognizing our identity in Christ helps us acknowledge our inherent value as children of God. It reassures us that we belong to the royal family of the King of Kings, which instills a sense of worth that is not dependent on external validation or societal standards.

2. Freedom from Condemnation: Understanding who we are in Christ liberates us from feelings of unworthiness and condemnation. The text emphasizes that our true identity is rooted in what Jesus says about us, rather than the lies and judgments of the enemy or others. This knowledge allows us to move forward without being held back by past mistakes or negative perceptions.

3. Empowerment to Live Authentically: Knowing our identity in Christ empowers us to live authentically. It enables us to embrace our quirks, flaws, and unique qualities, recognizing that God created us for a specific purpose. This authenticity allows us to engage with the world confidently, without the fear of comparison or judgment from others.

4. Guidance in Relationships: Understanding our identity in Christ helps us discern who is genuinely for us and who may seek to exploit our gifts. It enables us to establish healthier, more supportive relationships and to recognize those who celebrate our worth rather than diminish it.

5. Boldness in Facing Challenges: When we are grounded in our identity in Christ, we gain the boldness to stand firm in our beliefs and values, regardless of external opinions. This confidence allows us to respond to negativity or criticism with grace, reminding ourselves of our true worth.

6. Clarity in Purpose: Knowing our identity in Christ provides clarity about our purpose in life. It helps us understand the unique plans God has for us and encourages us to pursue those plans with confidence, knowing that we are equipped and called to fulfill them.

7. Healing and Restoration: The reassurance that God fills our empty places with His love, which is essential for healing and restoration. Understanding our identity in

Christ allows us to accept His love and grace, leading to personal transformation and wholeness.

In summary, understanding our identity in Christ is crucial for establishing self-worth, living authentically, navigating relationships, and confidently pursuing our God-given purpose. It serves as a foundation for healing and empowerment, enabling us to embrace the fullness of life that God has designed for us.

As we reflect on these truths, let us anchor ourselves in Scripture.

"Since then, you have been raised with Christ, set your hearts on things above, where Christ is, seated at the right hand of God. Set your minds on things above, not on earthly things. For you died, and your life is now hidden with Christ in God." — Colossians 3:1-3

"But you, LORD, are a shield around me, my glory, the One who lifts my head high." — Psalm 3:3

"I have told you these things, so that in me you may have peace. In this world, you will have trouble. But take heart! I have overcome the world." — John 16:33

By embracing your identity in Christ, you can walk confidently into the world, knowing that you are loved, valued, and destined for greatness. God fills the empty places with His love, and you are who He says you are. Let this truth guide you as you navigate life, empowering you to live fully and authentically as a child of the King.

Chapter Eleven
Finding Freedom from the Darkness

    This chapter holds a special place in my heart because I have personally struggled with depression and anxiety for most of my life. It wasn't until I began to delve into the realm of spiritual warfare that I discovered the existence of a demonic spirit often referred to as the spirit of depression and anxiety. I had no idea that my lifelong battles with depression were influenced by these demonic forces, which I had unwittingly opened myself up to. They were relentless in their torment, binding me until God intervened and began to deliver me from this darkness.

    At what I felt to be one of the lowest points of my life, I found myself at a crossroads, nearly ending my own life. It was a divine shaking that revealed to me the root of my struggles and what I needed to do to escape their grip. God began speaking to my heart, allowing me to see the true nature of what was happening in the spiritual realm.

To understand how to break free from depression and anxiety, we must first recognize the spiritual aspects at play. While some individuals experience depression due to chemical imbalances or emotional wounds from heartbreak, a significant element often overlooked is the influence of demonic spirits that seek to control our minds. Once these dark and negative entities filtrate our thoughts, they can saturate us with anxiety, guilt, regret, defeat, feelings of unworthiness, and hopelessness. This mental paralysis can lead us to shut down entirely.

So what can we do in a world that often feels nonfunctional? Too frequently, we find ourselves giving authority to these dark influences by resorting to destructive behaviors in a desperate attempt to elevate our serotonin levels. Many turn to alcohol, drugs, money, food, or sex as coping mechanisms. Unfortunately, this opens the door for a demonic entity that thrives on addiction, leading us further into a cycle of destruction. When the effects of these substances wear off, we often feel worse than before, plunging deeper into depression and anxiety. This cycle is what I refer to as "Satan's vortex," where one problem or addiction spirals into another, ultimately leaving us feeling like zombies, lacking feelings of Hope and Life.

But there is hope! Please take a moment to absorb these words, as this message is crucial for anyone grappling with these issues—or for those who love someone who is. This chapter is vital because the challenges we face as humans often culminate in feelings of depression and anxiety. We all experience these emotions at various points in our lives, and everyone deserves to know how to break free from them.

I remember being in a dark place not long ago, enveloped by gloom. The only way I could find temporary relief was through alcohol or antidepressants. I would dress up and go to clubs, attempting to mask my problems with distractions that only created more issues. There were times when I would stay in bed for a week, completely paralyzed by depression. The sunlight, when it streamed through the windows, felt painful to my eyes. I had become completely unaware of how far I had fallen.

Each time I mustered the strength to get up, I was met with the harsh reality of piled bills and dirty dishes, which only deepened my despair. The enemy orchestrated these circumstances to lure me in and push me to a point of no return. Trusting others became an impossibility after experiencing repeated hurt, leaving me feeling isolated and vulnerable.

You may relate to feelings of mistrust or disconnection from those around you. Perhaps your foundation has eroded little by little, leaving you feeling like a broken shell of your former self. The enemy's tactics are insidious; he makes your state of brokenness seem comfortable and familiar. Before you know it, the weight of overwhelming despair can paralyze you, leaving you unsure of how to recover.

Do any of these thoughts resonate with you?

- You believe your past mistakes are too numerous to recover from.
- You feel trapped in addiction, convinced that recovery is impossible.
- You are haunted by the loss of a loved one, believing you can never heal.
- You harbor resentment that consumes your heart, making forgiveness feel unattainable.
- You face false accusations that tarnish your reputation.
- You experience panic attacks following trauma.

- You've been hurt by someone in your church and struggle to return.
- You are overwhelmed by legal troubles and financial burdens.
- You feel your partner's love slipping away, fearing they will choose someone else.
- You've become so consumed by jealousy of the opposite sex that you neglect your children.
- You've seen your business decline and feel unappreciated at work.
- You are desperate for a job but feel stuck and unable to find one.
- You face impending financial crises and feel hopeless.
- You have gained weight and feel unattractive to the point of avoiding public spaces.
- You feel unattractive and believe no one will want to date or marry you because of your age.
- You fear you will be lonely forever or that you'll have to settle for a relationship that doesn't fulfill you.
- You think your family would be better off without you.

If you identify with any of these struggles, it's likely you are overwhelmed by stress, anxiety, and depression. I know this feeling well; I have walked that path and also witnessed friends experience similar turmoil. There were times I prayed for God to intervene magically, hoping He would resolve my problems instantaneously. After all, He is God and has the supernatural power to fix everything, right? The answer is yes, but He doesn't simply make the mess of our lives perfect overnight. Life was never perfect to begin with.

Even during my darkest moments—when I ignored calls from bill collectors, fought back against those who hurt me, and drowned my sorrows in alcohol—God was present. My eyes were focused on my problems rather than on Him. I had unwittingly attempted to take control of my life, which only led to a greater mess and a deeper fall into Satan's vortex.

But there is a way out!

"Humble yourselves, therefore, under God's mighty hand, that he may lift you up in due time. Cast all your anxiety on him because he cares for you." — 1 Peter 5:6-7

"The righteous cry out, and the LORD hears them; he delivers them from all their troubles." — Psalm 34:17

"I waited patiently for the LORD; he turned to me and heard my cry. He lifted me out of the slimy pit, out of the mud and mire; he set my feet on a rock and gave me a firm place to stand. He put a new song in my mouth, a hymn of praise to our God. Many will see and fear the LORD and put their trust in him." — Psalm 40:1-3

"For whatever is born of God overcomes the world; and this is the victory that has overcome the world—our faith." — John 5:4

By recognizing that we can cast our anxieties upon God, we find the hope and healing we so desperately seek. It takes humility and a willingness to surrender our struggles to Him. In doing so, we can begin to step out of the darkness and into the light that God has prepared for us. You are not alone, and with God's help, you can reclaim your life and your joy. Embrace this truth, and let it guide you toward healing and restoration.

Chapter Twelve
I Used to Be That Way, But Not Anymore!

    I want to share some powerful strategies that helped me tremendously in my battle against depression and anxiety. At one point in my life, I sought guidance from a pastor who was also a therapist. This pastor was one of the few who taught me how to fight the enemy with spiritual weapons. He introduced me to vital concepts that empowered me in my struggle against the demonic spirits that transported depression and anxiety.

    It was in my late 30s when I began to truly grasp these teachings, and they transformed my understanding of the battle I was facing. I discovered an inner strength I never knew I possessed, and now I want to pass these insights on to you. The purpose of this book is to share everything I learned, so you might not have to endure as much adversity before uncovering these truths.

    One of the first things the pastor gave me was a piece of paper outlining "31 Days to Your Pathway to

Freedom." I have committed these teachings to memory, as I relied on them repeatedly throughout my journey.

1.) Combating Negative Thoughts

The moment a negative thought or lie about yourself arises—perhaps a reminder of a past hurt, a temptation for revenge, or feelings of jealousy, fear, or sadness—immediately declare out loud:

"Thank You, Lord, for taking care of that! I am the daughter/son of the King of Kings. My Father will not allow this pain to continue. Satan, you have no authority in my life or over my mind anymore. My Father says that He who lives in me (God) is greater than he who lives in the world (Satan). Satan cannot get in my head any longer. These thoughts and lies from the enemy are null and void now. I used to think that way! I used to feel that way! I used to be that way, but not anymore! Thank You, Lord, for taking care of that!"

By failing to voice these affirmations, you inadvertently give the enemy the impression that he can continue to terrorize you.

When you find yourself speaking negatively about yourself or those around you, say out loud: "Cancel! I used to think that way! I used to feel that way! I used to be that way, but not anymore! Thank You, Lord, for taking care of that!"

2.) Daily Affirmations

Each night before bed and every morning upon waking, declare:

"I choose this day to trust in God! I choose life! I choose blessings! I walk in God's love! I walk in God's peace! I walk in God's glory! I walk in God's joy! I walk in God's hope! I walk in God's favor! I walk in God's wisdom! I walk in God's strength! I walk in God's vision! I walk in God's provision! I walk in God's courage! I walk in God's prosperity! I walk in God's divine healing! I walk in God's freedom!"

I know this may sound unconventional, but it truly works. There is immense power in our words. It took me years of skepticism and spiritual struggle before I embraced this truth. I often wished I could kick myself for wasting precious time resisting such a simple yet effective practice. If I had only recognized the power of speaking truth earlier, I could have defeated the enemy long ago instead of remaining stubborn and closed-minded.

As the Apostle Paul reminds us in Philippians 4:8:

"Finally, brothers and sisters, whatever is true, whatever is noble, whatever is right, whatever is pure, whatever is lovely, whatever is admirable—if anything is excellent or praiseworthy—think about such things."

By focusing our thoughts on what is true and good, we align ourselves with God's promises and empower ourselves to rise above the negativity and despair that once held us captive.

I wanted to share what I feel is the importance of speaking affirmations in the battle against depression and anxiety through several key points:

1. Immediate Response to Negative Thoughts: I encourage you to immediately counter negative thoughts or lies that arise in your mind with spoken affirmations. By vocalizing statements such as "Thank You, Lord, for taking care of that!" and asserting your identity as a child of God, you can reclaim your mental space and resist the influence of negative thoughts.

2. Establishing Authority Over Lies: By declaring that "Satan, you have no authority in my life or over my mind anymore," it highlights the power of affirmations in asserting control over one's thoughts and emotions. This empowers you to reject the lies the enemy tries to instill in your mind.

3. Creating a New Narrative: The repeated affirmations serve to create a new narrative in which you can redefine your self-perception. The phrases "I used to think that way! I used to feel that way! I used to be that way, but not anymore!" emphasize a transformation from a state of negativity to one of empowerment and hope.

4. Daily Practice: I want to suggest establishing a routine of speaking affirmations both at night before bed and in the morning upon waking. This regular practice reinforces positive beliefs and helps to maintain a mindset focused on trust, love, peace, and hope, which are essential for overcoming depression and anxiety.

5. Recognizing the Power of Words: I'd like to underscore the idea that there is significant power in the

words we speak. By initially dismissing this truth, I'd like to reflect on my
own journey of skepticism and the eventual realization that affirmations can lead to substantial change in one's mental state.

6. Biblical Foundation: I'd like to support the practice of affirmations with a biblical reference (Philippians 4:8), which encourages believers to focus on what is true and praiseworthy. This connection to scripture provides a spiritual foundation for the practice of speaking affirmations as a means of aligning one's thoughts with God's truth.

Overall, I felt the need to present affirmations as a proactive and essential tool in the fight against depression and anxiety, empowering everyone who is reading this to take control of your thoughts, reshape your identities, and ultimately find freedom from negativity.

In conclusion, remember: you have the power to change your narrative. You may have once struggled with feelings of unworthiness, depression, or anxiety, but by implementing these strategies, you can declare with confidence, "I used to be that way, but not anymore!" Embrace this journey of transformation, and let the truth of who you are in Christ guide you toward a brighter future filled with hope, joy, and freedom.

Chapter Thirteen
Declarations of Truth and Power

Throughout my years of working with teen girls and women, I often found that identity issues were caused by severe brokenness from abuse and hardships. I have witnessed the profound impact that pain and adversity can have on one's sense of self. These experiences often lead to insecurities that open the door for the enemy to wreak havoc in our lives. Today, I want to share a powerful set of declarations that can serve as a lifeline for all of God's children who are battling addiction, eating disorders, feelings of hopelessness, and the negativity of bullies who try to convince them that they are not enough etc…

This chapter is dedicated to those who are struggling with recovering from illness, disappointment, and heartbreak. It is for anyone who has loved friends only to find out they have turned their backs on you. It is for those who feel paralyzed by depression and anxiety. This chapter will serve those who are desperately trying to find hope again. Maybe you are mad at God. Maybe you have experienced poverty or someone close to losing their life. This chapter is for anyone needing a breakthrough. I am here to tell you that the enemy is full of lies and will use your heartbreak and vulnerability as a perfect opportunity to slip in your mind and create so many negative thoughts.

God made you perfectly, and He crafted just one of you for a reason. You are valued, intelligent, powerful and amazing! You are a shining light who overcomes and your comeback will be greater than your setback!

I invite you to read these declarations and identify with the ones that resonate with your heart. Speak them out loud with boldness, for there is incredible power in your words. It may feel strange at first, but you will be astounded by how declaring these truths can shift your life. The authority you possess through your spoken words is transformative—just give it a try!

CONFIDENCE

I am who God says I am.

He says I'm awesome! He says I'm beautiful, no matter what size my pants are.

He made me uniquely and perfectly for this world.

God designed me to be quirky, silly, funny, and bold.

As I grow older, I embrace the way I look.

-Proverbs 31:30 "Charm is deceitful, and beauty is vain, but a person who fears the LORD is to be praised."

STRENGTH

I am who God says I am.

I am a warrior NOT a worrier.

He has given me courage to fight battles sent to destroy me.

I am Strong!

I am resilient!

God has equipped me with everything I need to overcome any adversity that I face.

-Joshua 1:9 "Be strong and courageous. Do not be afraid; do not be discouraged, for the LORD your God will be with you wherever you go."

INSECURITY

I am perfectly and wonderfully made.

God did not make any mistakes while creating me.

I am no longer insecure.

I am beautiful!

I am worthy!

I am very intelligent!

I am free from judgment!

I forgive myself for seeing things negatively in myself that others don't notice and continually beating myself up mentally.

I am a child of the King of Kings and the Lord of Lords.

No weapon that the enemy throws at me will prosper.

-Isaiah 54:17 "No weapon that is fashioned against me shall succeed."

God tells me I'm worthy, so I believe Him.

I am more than good enough; I am qualified in every way.

I am walking in freedom.

I am strong.

I have wisdom.

I have an inheritance given to me from my Heavenly Father.

I do not identify with negative thoughts anymore.

What used to be my ceiling is now my floor.

God has given me authority and promotion that no man can give.

I will walk through life from this day forward, holding my head high.

I will use my past weaknesses to become my strength.

...In Jesus' Name, Amen.

HOPE

I am no longer bound to thoughts of hopelessness.

-Galatians 5:1 "It is for freedom that Christ has set me free."

I am no longer bound to addiction.

I am no longer bound to poverty.

I am no longer bound to confusion.

I am no longer bound to feelings of unworthiness.

God says I'm worthy, so I know I am worthy.

God says I'm free, so I know I am free.

I will walk in this freedom.

I will be strong.

I will never go backward, only forward.

In Jesus' Name, Amen!

ENEMIES

From this day forward, I will receive from the Kingdom of God, not the system of the earth.

-Matthew 6:9 "Do not lay up for yourselves treasures on earth, where moth and rust destroy and where thieves break in and steal."

I will no longer allow thoughts and lies from the enemy to worry me.

I will recognize that every negative thought is a lie meant to scare me or throw me off track.

-2 Corinthians 10:5 "We demolish arguments and every pretension that sets itself up against the knowledge of God."

I will trust in God's promises, knowing He never breaks them.

...In Jesus' Name, Amen!

TRUST

I declare that I will no longer dictate what victory should look like.

-Exodus 4:12 "Now go; I will help you speak and will teach you what to say."

I will follow the Holy Spirit and trust God's guidance.

He will never forsake or deceive me.

...In Jesus' Name, Amen!

PROSPERITY

God has made deliverance and prosperity for me!

I am the head and not the tail.

I have a seat at the table of abundance with the Lord.

I am a hard worker who has sown into the Kingdom of God.

God has watched me struggle and seen my hard work.

God has not forgotten me.

I will live a life of abundance.

-Deuteronomy 28:8 "The LORD will command the blessing upon me in my barns and in all that I put my hand to."

I will no longer doubt my worthiness.

In Jesus' Name, Amen!

TEMPTATION

I declare that I will no longer let temptation control me.

I will avoid temptation.

-Matthew 6:13 "Lead me not into temptation, but deliver me from the evil one."

When I face temptation, I will prove to myself how strong I am.

I have victory over temptation and have overcome it!!

In Jesus' Name, Amen!

WORTH

I declare that I am more than a conqueror!

Every lie and dart thrown at me by the enemy I bind and rebuke in the name of Jesus.

-Romans 8:37 "In all these things we are more than conquerors through him who loved us."

I will not allow my past to make me feel unworthy.

I am the Daughter/Son of The King of Kings.

I am highly favored in the Kingdom of God and in the flesh.

Blessings of finances, freedom, prosperity, love and wisdom are mine.

What I have gone through equips me to help others.

In Jesus' Name, Amen!

DISAPPOINTMENT

I declare that God has healed my heart!

-Psalm 34:18 "The Lord is near to the brokenhearted and saves the crushed in spirit."

The hurt I've experienced is a stepping stone to my testimony.

I will forgive those who disappointed me so I can be free.

I will be an example of how powerful the move of God is when moving forward after being disappointed.

I will trust God more than man from now on.

I will understand that if something doesn't work out that I was hoping for, God was protecting me from someone or something and I will be thankful.

I will have healthy relationships with those God brings into my life.

I am ready to walk in the promises of God, turning pain into gain.

In Jesus' Name, Amen!

HARD TIMES

I declare peace over my circumstances and finances!

-Ezekiel 37:1-14 speaks of a dry and desolate place in ones life, where is a miracle is required to restore life back into a lifeless circumstance. If the word of God says it then I trust it will be done.

-Proverbs 16:3 "Commit to the LORD whatever you do, and he will establish your plans."
I will defy the enemy's attempts to bring me down!
I will laugh when he says I should cry!
I trust God and know that abundance awaits me.
I declare that I am stepping into divine reversal!
The rest of my life will be the BEST of my life.
In Jesus' Name, Amen!

SUCCESS

I declare that I am blessed and highly favored!
I am seated in heavenly places.
No door that God opens for me will be shut by the enemy.
No door God closes for me will be opened by the enemy.
God will create Devine connections for me in my business life and personal life.
I will walk in abundance.
The ones who tried to sabotage my progress, prosperity and name will watch me become elevated and blessed.
-Proverbs 8:35

"For he who finds me finds life and obtains favor from the LORD."

I have found God!

In Jesus' Name, Amen!

ILLNESS

In Jesus' name, I declare illness to be gone!

-Exodus 23:25 "Worship the LORD your God, and his blessing will be on your food and water. I will take away sickness from you."

Every cell in my body is clean and healed!

I release miracles of healing in my body in the name of Jesus.

I declare that the test results come back negative on my behalf.

I believe God for miracles of healing in my life and in my family wherever I go.

Thank You, Lord, for healing me and delivering me from all sickness and all pain

God has given me authority over all sickness and disease therefore I'm taking that authority today and Declaring freedom from any sickness, pain and suffering.

I thank God for my healing, demonstrating my faith.

In Jesus' Name, Amen!

I AM BLESSED

I have authority through the blood of Jesus over my situation.

I am blessed and highly favored.

-Luke 12:7 says,

"Even the hairs of your head are all numbered. Fear not; you are of more value than many sparrows."

I will prosper and increase in number.

I will fill the earth and take charge of my roles and responsibilities on earth.

God has seated me in Heavenly places.

I am the head and not the tail.

What used to be my ceiling with any circumstance will now be my floor.

In Jesus' Name, Amen!

SEVERING UNGODLY TIES

I declare that today marks the beginning of my final breakthrough in severing ungodly soul ties that were bound to me by someone unworthy.

I declare that in this new place of my life, as I am moving forward, I will submit to God and have faith that he has me in his arms.

I will not go backwards in my walk to freedom, I will only move forward.

I will no longer be bound by thoughts of hurtful things that may cause me to want closure. God gave me closure by giving me freedom from the soul tie.

I will not try to keep in contact with the person God severed the soul tie from. I will not try to see what that person is doing or who they are congregating with. I will be okay with them moving forward without me.

I will no longer allow the enemy to cause me to go backwards by putting thoughts of "what if" in my head.

I will block any and all communication with the toxic person, place or thing that God has delivered me from.

I will not go backwards, only forward.

I will be expecting progress and prosperity while walking in my freedom from toxicity.

I will trust that God has better for me in my new season.

I will have boundaries from now on that will protect myself from ungodly soul ties.

I will ask God if a person, place or thing is good for me from now on so I don't make the same mistakes as I did in my past.

I deserve the feast and not the crumbs.

-2 Corinthians 6:14 says,

"Do not be unequally yoked with unbelievers."

I will create boundaries and stand firm in my identity as a child of the King!

In Jesus' Name, Amen!

IMPROVEMENT

I declare that I am anointed!

Today I will receive God's correction with humility and make adjustments that will cause my restoration to burst forth.

-Luke 4:18 "The Spirit of the Lord is upon me, because he has anointed me to proclaim good news to the poor."

Everything I do from now on will be infused with God's anointing!

In Jesus' Name, Amen!

DESERVING

I declare that my harvest is coming!

The favor of God comes toward me today

The Holy Spirit is guiding me into favorable pathways.

I believe in an exponentially magnanimous Father who loves me extravagantly, has every resource at his disposal for kingdom expansion through me, and whose generosity towards me knows no limitation

-Genesis 26:12 "Isaac sowed in that land and reaped in the same year a hundredfold. And the LORD blessed him."

I trust that my sacrifices have not gone unnoticed.
In Jesus' Name, Amen!

PROTECTION

I declare that angelic Hosts are camping out around me night and day protecting me from evil encounters!

I have authority by the blood of Jesus Christ over my situation.

I am protected!

I will be vindicated!

My words will be heard by those who can help me.

I declare that any accidents, adversity, attacks, and tragedies that we're headed my way are diverted right now.

I declare all attacks against myself and my loved ones will stop!

Divine appointments are on the way!

I declare that angels are carrying out the word of God on my behalf.

-Luke 4:10 "For it is written, 'He will command his angels concerning you.'"

I speak total peace and clarity over my life!

In Jesus' Name, Amen!

FEAR

I declare that today I will have the peace and boldness to give up what needs to be given up.

-Psalm 84:12 "Blessed is the one who trusts in you."

I know that FEAR is the opposite from FAITH.

From now on I will remember that only fear comes from thoughts that the enemy is giving me. Because the enemy is the author of lies then whatever I'm fearful of the opposite has to be true.

I trust the Lord and will no longer let fear hold me back from stepping into my freedom!

In Jesus' Name, Amen!

ADDICTION

Today I take full responsibility for attaining my goals and achieving fulfillment in a life free of substances or anything that may be binding me from moving forward in my prosperity and freedom.

-Proverbs 20:1
Wine is a mocker, strong drink a brawler,
and whoever is led astray by it is not wise.
-Proverbs 25:28
A man without self-control
is like a city broken into and left without walls.
-Jeremiah 17:14
Heal me, O LORD, and I shall be healed;
save me, and I shall be saved,
for you are my praise.

I declare that this week I am flexible enough to respond to change without any ungodly attachments binding me to my past.

I declare that any change I have to face is not frightening for me. I have not
been given a spirit of fear but of power, love and a sound mind.

I will accept the changes that I experience because they are opportunities for growth.

I choose to move forward trusting God and not man.

I will say no to things that will distract me from God's purpose for my life.

I feel powerful today because greater is He that is in me than he that is in the world.

The influence and impact I have on the world around me is greater than it has on me.

In Jesus name Amen!

This chapter serves as a powerful reminder of the declarations we can make to affirm our identities, strengths, and victories in Christ. By speaking these truths aloud, we can reclaim our power and embrace the abundant life God has planned for each of us. Let these declarations resonate in your heart and mind, and watch how they transform your life!

Chapter Fourteen
Keep Walking, There Is So Much More

One morning, as I sat in bed praying—something I often do upon waking—I felt an overwhelming heaviness in my heart. For years, I had struggled with suicidal thoughts, but that morning, the weight was particularly intense. Sadness, hopelessness, and a sense of defeat enveloped me, leaving me reluctant to leave the warmth of my covers. I just wanted to lay there and cry.

In my vulnerable state, I called out to God for help. After a moment of prayer, I found myself succumbing to tears, the emotions of depression and despair overtaking me. I made a decision to spend the entire day in bed, convincing myself to tell everyone I wasn't feeling well so they would leave me alone. I tried to drift back to sleep, hoping to silence the condemning voices and memories of failures that relentlessly echoed in my mind.

Then, unexpectedly, I was jolted by a voice. It was loud and clear, as if God were right there in the room with me. He commanded, "Get up! Get out of bed before you cause yourself more damage." I initially ignored it, dismissing the voice as my own internal struggle. "Just shut up," I thought, wanting nothing more than to fall back into sleep and escape it all.

But God persisted, "Mary, get up now! Get out of bed and put your clothes on! I'm telling you to get up. Bring a pen, your journal, and your Bible, and go to the bay where you can spend time with just me—no distractions."

Reluctantly, I climbed out of bed, grumbling as I got dressed. I drove to the bay, carrying my pad, pencil, and Bible. Before doing anything else, I prayed. It was then that God spoke again. He told me to take a walk with Him—not just a physical walk, but a spiritual one. He instructed me to document everything happening during this walk.

As I began to write, I quickly found myself stumped, unable to think of anything to say. God then urged me to put down the pencil and use my voice recorder to speak step by step through the experience.

I closed my eyes, and suddenly, I was transported back to my childhood. I envisioned myself as an eight-year-old girl—barefoot, with brown hair and hazel eyes—standing at the edge of a dark, foreboding woods.

Fear gripped me as I heard growls and howls from within, paralyzing me with terror.

At that moment, I saw God standing in the woods, extending His hand towards me. "Walk with me, daughter," He said. I shook my head in fear, trembling at the thought of stepping into the darkness. "The sharp pebbles will hurt my feet," I protested.

"Just take my hand and trust me," He reassured me. Gathering my courage, I took His hand and stepped onto the path. To my amazement, the sharp rocks transformed into soft, comfortable sand beneath my feet.

As we walked, the darkness around us began to dissipate, revealing a breathtaking transformation. The once menacing woods transformed into a vibrant, illuminated forest. The leaves and bushes glistened in vibrant greens, and everything appeared alive and healthy. Birds of extraordinary colors sang heavenly melodies, while butterflies flitted about, leaving trails of shimmering dust in their wake.

"Keep walking; there is so much more," God encouraged me. My heart swelled with joy as I marveled at the beauty unfolding before my eyes.

As we continued, a magnificent bird with wings that spanned as long as I was tall swooped down and perched on God's shoulder. I was awestruck, my eyes wide with disbelief. "WOW!" I exclaimed, my childlike wonder bubbling over.

After a short distance, I heard the gentle sound of a flowing stream. The sound harmonized with the birds' songs, creating a symphony of heavenly music. To the right of the path was a large rock beside the stream. God said, "Daughter, let's sit down and talk for a bit."

As we sat on the giant rock, He explained the significance of our journey. "Every step we take and every piece of nature you see is meaningful. This rock symbolizes me. I am your Rock during your weakest moments, providing the strength you need in times of adversity. This flowing water represents the living water you will find in me daily—always nourishing, never running dry. Like me, I will continuously flow through your life, helping you face every trial and battle. Your faith will grow deeper, just as the roots of the trees grow and are nourished by this stream."

Then, God took the eagle perched on His shoulder and placed it on mine. "This eagle symbolizes how I see you. You are strong and resilient, able to fly above the storm clouds and avoid the torrential downpours. You will always be protected from life's storms and will gain the ability to see the big picture. With eagle eyes, you will discern the enemy's tricks before they ensnare you, allowing you to soar above them."

After sharing this, the eagle took flight. God stood and took my hand, prompting me to walk further. Soon, we heard a loud roar—water cascading from the tallest, widest waterfall I'd ever seen. Despite the booming sound, I felt safe walking with God, trusting His protection.

"Come with me, beloved, and walk with me into this falling water," He invited. I followed, and miraculously, not a drop touched us. On the other side, we discovered an old treasure chest covered in moss.

"Go ahead, it's yours. Open it," God urged.

With all my might, I pushed the heavy lid open. The sight took my breath away: a treasure trove filled with the most exquisite jewels—rubies, emeralds, diamonds, sapphires, pearls, gold, and silver—all sparkling brilliantly. I dug my hands into the treasures, feeling the cool, smooth stones slip through my fingers. I was mesmerized, my heart full of joy as I looked up to see

God smiling with tears in His eyes, delighted at my excitement.

"This is all yours, and more," He said. "If you walk with me every day, you can experience this joy and treasure continuously."

After recording the details of this incredible walk, I opened my Bible to a random page. The first verse I saw was Proverbs 8:21: "Granting an inheritance to those who love me, and filling their treasuries." Then I turned to 2 Corinthians 4:6: "For God, who said, 'Let light shine out of darkness,' has shone in our hearts to give the light of the knowledge of the glory of God in the face of Jesus Christ."

Looking up, I smiled at the sky, feeling the gentle ocean breeze on my face, as if God were kissing me on my face. I noticed the flowers swaying in the same breeze, almost as if they were dancing. I smiled again, my heart bursting with gratitude. It was then that I realized it had been years that I had truly noticed such beauty.

Suddenly, everything felt brighter. The dim and cloudy veil that had shrouded my life lifted, revealing the vibrancy around me. At that moment, I realized that God had delivered me from my depression. By obeying His call to get up that morning and take a walk with Him, I had trusted Him to take away the pain and darkness. He replaced it with beauty, light, courage, and strength. It was as if His love had kissed my face, and the flowers danced in joyful celebration.

Psalm 40:1-3 says, "I waited patiently for the LORD; he turned to me and heard my cry. He lifted me out of the slimy pit, out of the mud and mire; he set my feet on a rock and gave me a firm place to stand. He put a new song in my mouth, a hymn of praise to our God. Many will see and fear the LORD and put their trust in him."

Deuteronomy 31:8 reassures us, "The LORD himself goes before you and will be with you; he will never leave you nor forsake you. Do not be afraid; do not be discouraged."

Keep walking, my friend. There is so much more waiting for you on the other side of your struggles. Embrace the journey, trust in His guidance, and watch as He transforms your life in ways you never thought possible.

Chapter Fifteen

Stepping Out of the Victim Garment

    As a child, I faced trauma after trauma that shaped my mindset into one of a victim. I grew up with experiences that were far from normal for most people, living a life that revolved around being victimized. It wasn't until I matured that I realized the depth of this mindset and how it impacted my ability to communicate and connect with those I loved. I had no idea how to address situations that made me uncomfortable or how to express my feelings without resorting to anger.

    When someone hurt me or made me feel threatened, I would go into a defensive mode. I had finally reached an age where I could take control of my life, and I did so by trying to dominate every situation. I was nice and accommodating until I sensed any potential for hurt, and that's when I would explode—cursing, screaming, and breaking things. I had mastered the art of delivering cutting remarks that could devastate those I cared about, leaving them wounded and me filled with guilt afterward.

I didn't realize at the time that I was allowing the enemy to manipulate my mind, keeping me bound in a cycle of pain and resentment. I clung to the memories of my childhood trauma, believing that my suffering entitled me to react however I wanted. The enemy whispered lies to me, encouraging me to retaliate and teach others a lesson. "You're an adult now," I would hear in my head, "Don't let anyone walk all over you. You have every right to fight back."

These thoughts were all designed to keep me trapped in a victim mentality feeling offended always and continue lashing out for revenge. When my boyfriend cheated on me, I would react by publicly shaming him on social media and spreading rumors, not caring about the damage I was inflicting. I realize now how deeply I was hurting inside, and how much authority I had given the enemy over my mind.

One day, after some reflection, I decided it was time to turn my life around. I began to seek the truth from God instead of listening to the enemy's lies. I learned that when I tried to teach others lessons or change their behavior, I was attempting to take on the role of God. Only He has the power to change hearts and lives. I realized that anger and revenge only lead to conflict, creating a toxic cycle of hurt that spiraled out of control.

Sure, people had hurt me. They had treated me unfairly and done unthinkable things. However, I discovered that walking with God gave me the self-control to step back and find peace in difficult situations. I learned to let go and trust Him to handle things. As an adult it was my responsibility to seek therapy and get mentally healthy and healed.

If I had truly known God and walked with him back then, I would have never allowed toxic people into my life to begin with. I would have known to guard my heart by putting up boundaries . I would have been more discerning about the relationships I formed, avoiding those drawn to me for superficial reasons. It's true what they say: toxic, broken people often attract one another. I was a mess, and it was time to own up to my role in that.

Looking back, I realized that part of the reason I attracted so many unhealthy people was because I myself was broken. Because I constantly whined about how horrible my life was and complained to everyone about the things others had put me through I was unknowingly putting vibrational energy into the atmosphere that attracted negative spiritual entities that were so easily welcomed into my world.

As a single mom who was always scraping by, I often shared my struggles, hoping for sympathy or help—a handout, a dream job, or a miracle that would suddenly lift me from my circumstances without putting in the work because I felt entitled because I was a victim of circumstances.

At times, I think I enjoyed playing the victim role because it garnered me attention and pity. I would pray to God, questioning why He allowed me to endure continuous hardships. Hardships that many times I welcomed into my life by making poor choices. For instance, I would give free hair services and makeovers to other single moms, thinking I was helping those in need, only to find out that many of them had more than I did and were simply looking for something for free. It never dawned on me that I should have asked God for discernment and been very careful who I spent my valuable time helping.

I was so focused on sharing my present and past pain, believing that it would elicit sympathy and perhaps prompt someone to help me escape my troubles. In reality, this behavior only fed into the enemy's plan to keep me trapped in my victim mindset. I remained stuck in the muck of my own negativity, speaking endlessly about poverty and gloom.

I had no idea how powerful our words truly are. People would occasionally tell me to speak positively over my life, but I never felt positive, so why should I pretend? It wasn't until I began learning more about spiritual warfare that the truth began to resonate.

I discovered that we can actually speak things into existence—both positively and negatively. By voicing negativity, I inadvertently gave the enemy authority to manifest the very things I spoke about. I realized that as long as I identified as a victim and continued to vocalize that identity, I would remain a victim.

So, I began to shift my mindset. Even if I didn't immediately see changes for the better, I reminded myself that God is the God of unbroken promises, and He was going to set me free. I focused on strengthening my faith and began telling the enemy to back off; he was no longer welcome in my life. When the enemy whispered lies about my supposed destiny of gloom and poverty, I reminded myself that I am a daughter of the King, and my inheritance is one that a daughter of a King would have. I understood that doubting this was putting God in a box and demonstrating my lack of faith.

It dawned on me that we are all God's children, and He desires for us to prosper. He grants us free will, and when we take matters into our own hands, walking without Him, we must accept the consequences of our choices. We have the choice to walk with Him and experience peace during adversity. We can choose to believe God or the enemy regarding who we are and what we deserve.

I began to see myself as a warrior and a conqueror rather than a weak-minded victim. I recognized the challenges I had faced and became proud of myself for overcoming them, rather than lamenting how others had wronged me. I started to see that some of my past experiences had actually saved my life, making me stronger and building my character. As I embraced this perspective, I noticed a significant turnaround in my life.

Our positive words and unwavering faith activate blessings and divine turnarounds. It amazed me how quickly things began to shift once I made this change. It truly is that simple. We must humble ourselves enough to acknowledge our past mistakes and learn from them.

Accepting responsibility allows us to break free from the cycle of victimhood.

What does this realization say about us? Perhaps it suggests that we are not as much of a victim as we once thought. Maybe we were willing participants in the dynamics of our relationships. Recognizing our faults is crucial before we can address the problems and make meaningful changes. While we may not be the reason someone hurt us, we are responsible for how we choose to deal with that hurt.

We need to be vigilant in recognizing red flags and leaving toxic situations before they take root. Life is a continuous learning process. You can't address a problem without getting to its root. Just as you can't stop a weed from growing without pulling it out by the roots, you cannot conquer adversity without confronting the underlying issues. Until we acknowledge our role in perpetuating cycles of pain, we will remain stuck in patterns that keep us from moving forward.

I have a dear friend who is a survivor of human trafficking. She has taught me a great deal about the transformative power of words and mindset. After enduring unimaginable horrors—being drugged, raped, and tortured—she was finally rescued. One day, while doing her hair and makeup to help her feel beautiful, I told her how amazing and strong she was after everything she had endured. I asked, "What is it like being a trafficking victim?"

She quickly corrected me, saying, "I am not a victim anymore. People who survive human trafficking hate being called victims. We are survivors. By labeling us as victims, you are insinuating that we are still being victimized."

Her words struck a chord within me. She explained that holding onto the victim's identity meant harboring pain, resentment, and toxic feelings. "I chose to be a survivor," she said. "I didn't want to live in fear, hurt, or defeat anymore. I am now brave, healed, and victorious."

That conversation opened my eyes to the reality of stepping out of a victim identity and embracing the bold, new warrior identity that God intended for me. The enemy wants to keep us feeling like victims because he knows that as long as we cling to that identity, we will never prosper.

So, I began to surrender everything that had hurt me to God. I handed over all the negative feelings and thoughts that clouded my mind. I stepped out of the victim's garment and into the armor of God. There is incredible power in this transformation.

As we move forward, let us embrace the identity of a survivor, a warrior, and a victor. In doing so, we can break free from the chains of our past and walk confidently into the future that God has prepared for us.

Once I gained wisdom and began to understand how to fight spiritually, I took responsibility by taking the following steps and more to break free from the victim mentality:

1. Stop Feeding the Victim Mentality: I quit wallowing in self-pity. I stopped talking all the time about how badly I had been treated and made a conscious decision to give up the victim mentality.

2. Remove Toxic Influences: I blocked and deleted toxic people from my life. It was difficult because I cared for them, but I knew it was necessary for my healing.

3. Forgive and Pray: I forgave those who had hurt me and prayed for their freedom, just as I sought my own.

4. Refuse to Engage in Drama: I stopped participating in situations that fueled conflict. I learned that drama grows when you feed it. Instead of trying to control everything, I realized I was being manipulated by the enemy. I needed to trust God to handle the situation. I realized how I was wasting precious time concentrating on the toxic negativity.

5. Let God Be God: I surrendered my need to have the last word. I allowed God to take control and guide me. He would vindicate me.

6. Stop Seeking Validation: I ceased trying to make others understand my pain or force apologies that never came. I recognized the futility of these actions.

7. Embrace Victory Over Victimhood: Instead of punishing others for my pain, I gave everything to God, allowing myself to transform from a victim to a victor. I became a survivor!

8. Empathy Over Malice: I learned not to take joy in another's suffering, understanding that they, too, have

been broken. They also belong to God. He loves them just as much as He loves me.

9. Trust in God's Justice: I came to understand that God deals with everyone according to His justice, not our human desires. God knows what we've all faced and been traumatized with since birth. God knows our hearts and the thought process behind everything we do.

By taking these steps, I began to dismantle the victim mentality that had held me captive for so long. I learned to embrace my identity as a beloved child of God, empowered to forge a new path filled with hope, healing, and love. The journey wasn't always easy, but it was profoundly transformative. As I continued to walk with God, I discovered there was so much more to life than living in the shadows of my past. I learned to step into the light and live fully as the victor I was meant to be.

Revelation 3:21
He who overcomes, I will grant to him to sit down with Me on My throne, as I also overcame and sat down with My Father on His

throne.

Philippians 4:13
I can do all things through Him who strengthens me.

1 John 5:4
For whatever is born of God overcomes the world; and this is the victory that has overcome the world--our faith.

1 Corinthians 15:57
But thanks be to God, who gives us the victory through our Lord Jesus Christ.

Romans 8:37
But in all these things we overwhelmingly conquer through Him who loved us.

Revelation 6:2
I looked, and behold, a white horse, and he who sat on it had a bow; and a crown was given to him, and he went out conquering and to conquer.

Chapter Sixteen
The Power of Forgiveness

One profound realization I had while growing closer to God was the importance of the commandment to "Love Thy Neighbor." I admit, I understand how challenging it can be to love certain people. We all have someone in our lives we might prefer to avoid entirely—those who stir up drama or have wronged us in significant ways. How can we possibly love someone who has stolen from us, spread lies, or caused us deep pain? The answer lies in forgiveness.

Forgiveness is the key to our own healing, and we cannot genuinely forgive without the strength that God provides. He doesn't expect us to carry out His commands alone; He knows our limitations. This is why He invites us to take His hand and walk this journey together. Only God can turn what seems impossible into reality. When we follow Christ, our human logic often fades away because God is a God of miracles. By walking with Him, we find it easier to adhere to His teachings, enabling us to love and forgive even those who have hurt us deeply.

We all fall short and act in ways that make us unworthy of God's love. Yet, despite our flaws, God affirms our worthiness. Jesus sacrificed Himself, enduring ridicule and humiliation to demonstrate how valuable we are, even when we feel unlovable. Importantly, God doesn't expect us to forgive those who have wronged us in our own strength. When we walk with Him, He transforms our minds to be more aligned with His. It is only through Him that we can achieve this level of forgiveness, and it can happen when we allow Him to work through us.

Now that I have committed to walking with Christ, my perspective has shifted dramatically. Instead of seeking revenge on those who wronged me, I now pray for them—even for those who tried to destroy my reputation. By choosing to align my thoughts with God's, I have witnessed miraculous changes in my life. I now see people through Jesus's eyes. Instead of dwelling on their faults, I have compassion for them, recognizing that their hurtful actions often stem from their own pain and trauma.

Some people may not comprehend the spiritual battles that are very real in our lives. They may not realize how the enemy uses our past experiences against us. Regardless of the reasons behind others' actions, we must forgive them to release ourselves from the heaviness of their transgressions. When we relinquish that pain to God, it no longer burdens us.

Does forgiving someone mean we must allow them to hurt us again? Absolutely not. Forgiveness is about freeing ourselves, not about enabling further harm. However, when we forgive and pray for those who hurt us, we invite God to work in both their hearts and ours. We give God the opportunity to change their past and future circumstances, as He does for us.

No one person is better than another in the eyes of God. He grants us favor when we choose to walk with Him. Just as a mother rewards her daughter with privileges for obedience, God rewards us for choosing to follow Him, even when it's difficult. But He loves all His children equally.

The most significant reason God instructs us to forgive is that forgiveness breaks ungodly yokes that hinder our progress in life. A yoke represents something that binds us together or holds us back. Many of us carry yokes formed in childhood that cannot be broken until we take authority over them. The Bible tells us to forgive, but it also reveals why this act is crucial. Holding onto resentment has deep repercussions, while forgiveness opens the door to healing.

Forgiving means trusting God to handle the situation in His way. We trust Him to heal our hearts, which cannot mend while we cling to pain and bitterness. The incredible part of forgiveness is that it brings blessings and freedom. God never asks us to give something to Him without returning something even greater to us.

Forgiveness is vital for our liberation. We must also recognize that while forgiving others is powerful, the most critical forgiveness we often need to extend is to ourselves. Many of us carry burdens from past actions that the enemy relentlessly brings up, using them to keep us trapped in guilt.

Perhaps you have made choices you regret—maybe you had an abortion, harmed someone, Caused pain from your past addiction to sex or substances, or neglected your child. The enemy wants you to cling to that guilt, convincing you that you deserve bad things in your life. He will lie to you, making you feel unworthy of walking with God, even as you grow spiritually and mentally. The enemy thrives on keeping you distant from God, manipulating you with feelings of unworthiness.

But God made sure you are reading this message today to remind you just how worthy you truly are. Nobody is worthy without Him; however, because Jesus died for us, we can put our past behind us and walk in freedom. By following the steps outlined below, you can break the yokes the devil has bound you with and experience miraculous healing and the power to move forward. God is ready to accelerate you into a new season of prosperity.

1. Pray for Forgiveness: Ask God to forgive you for the things you have done to others. Reflect and think of everything from which you need forgiveness.

2. Release Pain: Pray about giving to God the hurt caused by others and forgive each person involved. Hand over that pain to Him.

3. Forgive Yourself: Pray for God to remove the guilt associated with your past actions and then forgive yourself. When the enemy tries to fill your mind with condemnation, take authority over those thoughts.

Remind both yourself and the enemy that you do not walk in the flesh but in the Spirit, and trust that the Spirit will guide you. By trusting in this spiritual journey, you can have confidence that Jesus has your back. If God equipped David to conquer Goliath, He has also equipped and cleaned you up to face your own giants. The enemy's weapons are spiritual, and God tells you that forgiveness is your sword, which He is sharpening. By listening to Him and rebuking the lies of the enemy, you can rest assured that no weapon formed against you will prosper.

Walking in the flesh means relying on your own strength. When you walk with God, you release the flesh and embrace the Spirit. God will always lead your steps and sharpen your sword. We all make mistakes, but God does not. The more forgiveness we extend, the closer we draw to Him, and the easier our battles become.

Be confident in knowing that Christ is fighting the good fight for you. What was once a mess in your life can turn around. Do not identify with condemnation; identify only with victory. See your victory before you experience it, for that is how you demonstrate the magnitude of your faith. God responds more swiftly to those who have unwavering faith. He is the God of unbroken promises, and He will come through for you.

Colossians 3:13
Bear with each other and forgive one another if any of you has a grievance against someone. Forgive as the Lord forgave you.

Ephesians 4:31-31-
Get rid of all bitterness, rage and anger, brawling and slander, along with every form of
malice.
32 Be kind and compassionate to one another, forgiving each other, just as in Christ God forgave you.

Hebrews 10:17
Then he adds: "Their sins and lawless acts
I will remember no more."

Daniel 9:9
The Lord our God is merciful and forgiving, even though we have rebelled against him.

Mark 11:25
"And when you stand praying, if you hold anything against anyone, forgive them, so that your Father in heaven may forgive you your sins."

Colossians 2:13-15

When you were dead in your transgressions and the uncircumcision of your flesh, He made you alive together with Him, having forgiven us all our transgressions, having canceled out the certificate of debt consisting of decrees against us, which was hostile to us; and He has taken it out of the way, having nailed it to the cross. When He had disarmed the rulers and authorities, He made a public display of them, having triumphed over them through Him.

Chapter Seventeen
Ungodly Soul Ties

 I finally made the difficult decision to step out of a relationship with the man I believed was the love of my life. It was the hardest choice I have ever had to make. The pain it caused tore me apart from the inside out. I had always felt that he was my soulmate; my love for him ran deep. I thought the intensity of our passion was a sign that God had brought us together. Little did I know, I was being deceived by the enemy—what I believed was a divine connection was actually a pathway to destruction.

 I tried everything to make the relationship work, clinging to a vision of him overcoming his addictions and becoming the man I always knew he could be. I held onto the hope that my love and dedication would provide him with the strength to persevere and ultimately become the husband I dreamed he would be. Our relationship was so toxic that we broke up every few weeks, only to rekindle things shortly after. This cycle continued for about eight years. I can only imagine how frustrating my back-and-forth behavior must have been for my friends. One moment I loved him, and he seemed like a good man; the next, I was venting to them about how horrible he was. I would claim he was cheating, only to later insist that I had been misled by someone trying to break us apart.

Reflecting on this now drives me to distraction. When I broke up with him, I would share all of his weaknesses and problems with anyone who would listen. I felt the need to retaliate by engaging in mean, vindictive behavior because he was spreading lies about me, particularly to his female friends. It was exhausting. I remember how obsessed I became, fixating on what he was doing and who he was talking to. I scrutinized his Facebook page, analyzing who liked his comments and what he said.

I know, it all sounds ridiculous and juvenile, but it was my reality. I was deeply hurt and had fallen into a trap set by the enemy, focusing solely on drama to the detriment of my relationship with God. I had become a stalker and a victim, obsessed with everything except what truly mattered.

In my determination to catch him in the act, I often screamed at my children to not interrupt me during my investigations or arguments with him. The enemy had me right where he wanted, using my desire for control to distract me from my responsibilities. I would leave clients in the salon to argue with him, even neglecting their hair processing, risking damage. I was spiraling into darkness, completely unaware of how my world was crumbling around me. My life revolved around a man, not God.

I remember receiving a book about breaking ungodly soul ties, and it was a revelation. Every page resonated with my life, as if the author had written it specifically for me. It marked a significant turning point. God revealed to me that I had been ensnared by numerous demonic influences. The concept of soul ties suddenly made sense. When we create ungodly soul ties with someone, we often begin to adopt their behaviors, which may have originated from others. This process doesn't happen overnight, but over time, it leads to an unstable relationship under the authority of the Prince of Darkness.

I had never struggled with alcohol or pornography until I formed these ungodly ties with my ex. I don't blame him for the chaos in my life; I acknowledge that I strayed from God and allowed the enemy to infiltrate my thoughts and actions. My poor choices distorted my view of reality, leaving me feeling hurt, entitled, and perpetually victimized.

I spoke incessantly about my misfortunes, which only solidified my victim mentality. I was complacent in my suffering. But God was there, walking me through it all. I never completely turned my back on Him, even as I engaged in sinful behavior. I still listened for His voice, and He spoke to me during prayer, urging me to leave the relationship. He made it clear that my ex's brokenness and my own were fueling our destructive cycle. God impressed upon my heart that two broken people cannot grow positively together; we only project our pain onto each other, causing more damage.

As I cried in the shower, pleading for relief from my heartache, God guided me. He told me to reflect on all the people with whom I had shared sexual relationships or emotional attachments. I needed to ask Him to break any ungodly ties and yokes I may have inherited from them. Believe it or not, breaking these ties only takes a few seconds, while the pain and addiction can linger for years.

To experience true freedom, we must allow God to work in our lives. The closer we draw to Him, the clearer our discernment becomes. We cannot be set free until we sever all ungodly ties.

It was a grueling process, but I made the choice to distance myself from the man I had once called the love of my life. I moved out of state, recognizing that every time we broke up, something would inevitably pull us back together. It was akin to any addiction; once you commit to cutting something out of your life, temptations arise that make it easy to fall back into old patterns. I understood this, so I packed my belongings and relocated.

It was the hardest decision I had ever made—cutting ties with someone I desperately loved. However, after eight years of turmoil, I knew the relationship was not ordained by God. It took me a year to stop crying over my decision, especially when I received emails from him expressing his continued love and longing for me. I often questioned whether I had made the right choice. Nevertheless, I recognized that this decision was necessary for both of us to move forward. My pain and anger were only exacerbating his brokenness.

Around this same time frame I also had a friend whom I once considered my best friend. However, as I grew closer to God, I began to see the truth of our relationship. I realized her behavior kept me bound as I constantly felt the need to prove myself to her. Our friendship was fraught with drama, and I found myself defending my loyalty against baseless accusations. At that point, I recognized that her negativity was a distraction from my relationship with God, and I severed that tie as well. I thought soul ties could only be with a man until realizing that An ungodly soul tie can be with any person, place or thing that you feel codependent with. Anything taking hold of your soul as if it is a part of you. Soul ties are not always ungodly. You can have a soul tie that is good. For instance, we may have them with family or our spouse etc...

The sooner you can identify counterfeit friends and toxic people in your life, the quicker you can break free from the burdens they impose. Unnecessary strife holds you back from necessary healing and breakthroughs. We often overlook the red flags that God tries to show us about people at the start of a relationship. We can be so easily fooled by charm and appearances that we believe we can change their toxic behavior through our love.

But the truth is, we are not equipped to change anyone—only God can do that. When we attempt to change someone, we are stepping into God's role, and we will inevitably face disappointment. In reality, we often end up being the ones who change, typically for the worse.

Ask yourself:

- Where you once smiled, are you now crying all the time?

- Where you once laughed and enjoyed life, do you now seclude yourself and feel insecure?

- Did you used to have meaningful conversations with friends and family, and now find yourself feeling depressed and angry?

The spirits influencing the destruction in others' lives can begin to manifest in yours as well. Whether it's a friend or lover, you must break those ties to become the person God has called you to be.

I know this all sounds overwhelming, but it did to me too until I realized the truth of these teachings. I trusted my God and what he was showing me through words in the Bible. I knew that since I had a relationship with God and understood him more clearly, that the words in the Bible would make more sense. I believed it contained wisdom, but much of this felt foreign to me. That was until I conducted my own research, discovering scriptures that illuminated the spiritual warfare I was facing. I recognized that my unhappiness stemmed from soul ties and generational behaviors. I understood that my failure to follow God's guidance had allowed chains of despair to chip away at my heart and soul.

Breaking these ungodly ties creates breakthroughs that enable you to pursue the dreams you may have abandoned—dreams that God has placed in your heart. Your calling is unique to you, but the enemy knows how to distract you. He will use things that appear good.

I urge each of you reading this book to conduct your own research on ungodly soul ties, yokes, and generational behaviors. You'll find truths that have been withheld from you—truths that the enemy has tried to keep you from discovering your entire life. Many churches focus on topics that may not adequately address the battle against Satan.

I've spoken to church staff members who had no idea what I was discussing when I asked about these matters. The first church that truly opened my eyes to this was Worship With Wonders in Kennesaw, Georgia. God was already revealing these truths to me, and the pastors confirmed what He had been telling me. I am eternally grateful for their obedience to God, even when others may have viewed them as eccentric—as I once did.

They showed me the truth, and I am writing this book to share that truth with you so that you too can experience freedom. The Bible speaks extensively about generational curses and soul ties. Although the term "soul ties" is not specifically mentioned, the Bible refers to souls being knit together and becoming one flesh, as well as ungodly yokes. These yokes cannot be broken unless you take authority over them.

The Bible instructs us to forgive, but it also emphasizes the importance of understanding why forgiveness is essential. Many people hastily tell you what God expects without explaining the reasons behind His commands.

While God has established rules for us to follow, it can be challenging to adhere to them without understanding the rationale behind them. We live in a world where some people identify as Christians yet focus on condemning others rather than sharing God's love. This approach reminds me of my stepdad, who would yell at me for making mistakes without explaining why his anger was warranted.

God is not a figure who seeks to control us; He genuinely loves us and desires for us to reciprocate that love. We cannot expect those who know nothing of God's love to adhere to His commands. Many leaders fail to instruct non-believers in what is truly happening in their lives and how it relates to God's truth.

Belief in God and knowing Him are two separate concepts. We must strive for a genuine friendship with Him. Remember, God meets us where we are; He does not expect us to ascend to His heavenly level. Instead, He walks alongside us to guide us toward our destination. During this journey, we must heed His instructions, as they will protect us from harm. God will break the ties and behaviors that bind us, leading us to freedom. We cannot achieve this without Him.

Some examples of generational behaviors and soul ties include:
- Depression and anxiety
- Victim mentality
- Entitlement issues
- Substance abuse (drugs and alcohol)
- Sexual addictions

- An unhealthy desire to help others at our own expense
- Generational illnesses (such as cancer or diabetes)
- Gluttony
- Neglecting family for work
- Gossiping
- Superficiality
- Lying
- Feelings of defeat
- Child abuse
- Hoarding
- Unreliability
- Lack of loyalty
- Prostitution
- Money-driven behavior
- Pride and ego
- Bullying, etc.

There are countless more examples. You can likely identify behaviors that are unhealthy and trace them back to generational patterns or close relationships. If you do not address these, you risk passing them onto your children, perpetuating destructive cycles.

If you are serious about breaking free from these chains, I encourage you to visit the prayer section at the back of this book and recite one of the prayers designed to sever demonic ties and start anew. Take authority over each situation and addiction. Command these influences to leave—do not ask or beg. God has granted you the authority to expel these spirits. They must obey when you invoke Jesus' name.

Name each issue and command it to depart in Jesus' name. They will flee. However, you must not allow them to return, for the Bible warns that they will come back sevenfold if given the chance. This means cutting off friendships and relationships with anyone harboring similar spirits. You cannot be strong enough to be around these individuals until you have healed and learned how to fight back with the spiritual sword.

Tricks the Enemy May Use:

1. The enemy may convince you that you are meant to be with someone or that you need something you can't stop thinking about. He might even make you believe that God has placed these people or things in your life.

2. We may feel compelled to help broken individuals because it feels right.
   - However, we cannot help anyone until we have healed ourselves.
   - We cannot love anyone authentically until we love ourselves first.
   - God would never allow someone to enter our peaceful lives only to bring chaos and destruction.
   - Getting angry because we cannot change someone or because they won't change is akin to being frustrated with a deaf person for their inability to hear. It is futile to expect someone to understand something they cannot grasp.

3. If you find yourself in a constant cycle of arguing and reconciling with someone, it is likely not a God-given relationship.
   - You may experience fleeting happiness, but if the pain consistently outweighs the joy, it is not of God.
   - God does not place us in harmful situations; instead, He transforms those situations into beauty, aligning them with His divine plan.

4. If you find yourself obsessing over someone or something, you likely have an ungodly soul tie. God is a jealous God; He would never place someone or

something in your life that you would prioritize over Him.

5. If you manipulate or lie to change someone, it is a clear indication of an ungodly soul tie.

Try Something Different:

1. If you've attempted to distance yourself from a person or situation but still feel bound, try a different approach. Stay away from them completely and surrender everything to God.

2. Spend your weekends at home, focusing on strengthening your relationship with God instead of discussing your troubles with everyone else.

   - God will provide you with peace that people cannot.

3. Dispose of anything symbolic of the ties you wish to sever. Give these items to a friend to store away so you are not continually reminded or tempted.

4. Once you allow God to cleanse the remnants of these soul ties, do not return to the situation that once held you captive.

   - Be aware that the enemy is cunning and will approach you from new angles to entice you back into old patterns. Stay vigilant.

5. Maintain a close relationship with God, who will grant you discernment to recognize the enemy's attempts to sneak back into your life.

- The Bible warns that when a demon leaves a person, it may wander in search of rest, but upon finding none, it will return to the individual. If it finds the heart unoccupied—because it has not been filled with Godly things—it will bring seven more malevolent spirits to dwell within, leaving the person worse off than before.

6. When you obsess over or idolize someone or something, you open yourself up to ungodly spirits attached to that person or thing. You create an idol out of them, and God never places you in such a predicament.

Scriptural References:

- Deuteronomy 5:9: "Thou shalt not bow down thyself unto them, nor serve them: for I the LORD thy God [am] a jealous God, visiting the iniquity of the fathers upon the children unto the third and fourth generation of them that hate me."

- Matthew 5:30: "And if thy right hand offends thee, cut it off, and cast [it] from thee: for it is profitable for thee that one of thy members should perish, and not that thy whole body should be cast into hell."

- 2 Corinthians 6:14: "Be ye not unequally yoked together with unbelievers: for what fellowship hath righteousness with unrighteousness? and what communion hath light with darkness?"

- 1 Corinthians 6:16: "What? Know ye not that he which is joined to a harlot is one body? For two, saith he, shall be one flesh."

- Exodus 20:5: "Thou shalt not bow down thyself to them, nor serve them: for I the LORD thy God [am] a jealous God, visiting the iniquity of the fathers upon the children unto the third and fourth generation of them that hate me."

- Jeremiah 17:5: "Thus saith the LORD; Cursed [be] the man that trusteth in man, and maketh flesh his arm, and whose heart departeth from the LORD."

- Deuteronomy 13:6: "If your brother, the son of your mother, or your son or your daughter or the wife you embrace or your friend who is as your own soul entices you secretly, saying, 'Let us go and serve other gods, which neither you nor your fathers have known.'"

- Ephesians 6:12: "For we wrestle not against flesh and blood, but against principalities, against powers, against the rulers of the darkness of this world, against spiritual wickedness in high places."

- Numbers 14:18: "The LORD [is] longsuffering, and of great mercy, forgiving iniquity and transgression, and by no means clearing [the guilty]; visiting the iniquity of the fathers upon the children unto the third and fourth generation."

- Exodus 23:30: "And I will drive out the nations before thee, and enlarge thy borders: neither shall any man desire thy land, when thou shalt go up to appear before the LORD thy God thrice in the year."

Through this journey of recognizing and breaking ungodly ties, you will find healing, freedom, and a renewed sense of purpose. Remember, God is with you every step of the way, guiding you toward the life He has destined for you. Embrace the journey, and allow Him to lead you into the fullness of His love and grace.

Chapter Eighteen
Discerning Between Good and God-Ordained

On my journey to self-help and freedom, I was constantly distracted by wondering if the people, places, or things I chose were from God. I found that the more I wanted to stay on the right track and not slip backward, the more options I had, which only added to my confusion. Not everything that appears good in our lives is necessarily aligned with God's divine purpose. A promising job offer, a seemingly perfect relationship, or a personal milestone can all be classified as "good" but may not be part of God's plan for us.

The reality is that there are countless good things we can pursue. In fact, having too many options can create challenges in our lives in two significant ways. First, we might overcommit ourselves, spreading our energy too thin and ultimately failing to excel in anything. Alternatively, when faced with an overwhelming array of choices, we may find ourselves paralyzed by indecision, unable to choose any path at all.

This is where discernment becomes essential. Just because an opportunity is good does not automatically mean it is what God desires for us. As Voltaire wisely noted, "The enemy of the best is the good." The crucial question is: "What has God truly called us to do?" It's important to remember that just because an option presents itself doesn't obligate us to accept it. While it's beneficial to seek godly counsel when new opportunities arise, we often fall into the trap of overthinking. We can find ourselves caught in a mental whirlwind, cycling through "what ifs" and "but thens," exhausting ourselves with possibilities until we've reasoned ourselves into confusion.

Wouldn't it be nice if we could just receive a clear sign from heaven? A bright neon arrow saying, "Go this way!" to guide us through the maze of choices?

However, we must be vigilant. The enemy is a master manipulator. He knows better than to tempt those who are genuinely seeking to follow God with blatant acts of rebellion. Look at how he tempted Christ in the wilderness: he offered Him "good" things, like bread to satisfy His hunger and the chance to showcase His divine power. While these options weren't inherently sinful, they would have been a violation of God's plan for Jesus.

So how can we discern what is truly from God?

A good idea often feels thrilling and aligns with our inner desires, but a God idea is a calling planted within us by the Holy Spirit—one that has the potential to create a kingdom impact and carry significant weight. Distinguishing between the two can be challenging, and it's easy to conflate good things with God-ordained purposes. We may find ourselves elevating good gifts—such as food, relationships, culture, and nature—into positions of undue importance, inadvertently pushing God aside.

God has indeed blessed us with many wonderful things: delicious food, joyful companionship, vibrant cultures, and the beauty of nature. Yet, the enemy excels at using these very blessings to distract us from our Creator. The Bible warns us in 1 Peter 5:8, "Be self-controlled and alert. Your enemy the devil prowls around like a roaring lion looking for someone to devour." When we become so engrossed in enjoying these gifts—even expressing gratitude for them—we risk becoming numb to the reality that they can easily morph into idols in our lives.

We often overlook the subtle ways in which we might idolize the good things around us. Perhaps we haven't paused to reflect on whether we've elevated our new romantic partner to an unhealthy status. Or maybe we haven't considered if we're idolizing our children, placing undue expectations or significance on them.

In our journey of faith, it is crucial to recognize the difference between what is merely good and what is divinely ordained by God. By doing so, we can avoid the pitfalls of distraction and ensure that our lives are aligned with His purpose. Ultimately, we must be intentional in our choices, seeking not only the good but also the God-ordained paths that lead to fulfillment and purpose in our lives.

If it's merely a good thing, be cautious, because the enemy often disguises his traps as good opportunities. When we drift away from God, we stop seeking His guidance, leaving gaps that can easily be filled with deception. The enemy places "good things" in our paths to set us up for destruction, making us regress in our spiritual journey.

If you discover that you've been deceived, simply pick yourself up, begin praying about every aspect of your life you need guidance for, and trust that God will remove unworthy things, relationships, and circumstances. He will realign your path and continue to bless your journey.

Chapter Nineteen
The Importance of Good and Solid Relationships

    Life is full of unexpected twists and turns, and people inevitably make mistakes, regardless of their character. As we navigate our paths, we may find ourselves reflecting on a rocky past filled with challenging circumstances. For me, the longing for a father figure in my childhood influenced my choices in adulthood. In my quest for validation, I often chose relationships with men who disrespected me, valuing me only for my appearance or sex. In my twenties, I found myself working in strip clubs, believing that by commodifying my body, I could gain the attention and affirmation I desperately sought. I thought that by embracing my sexuality, I would finally feel worthy of love and acceptance.

    Looking back, I recognize the poor decisions I made and the significant lessons I learned from the school of hard knocks. Should I carry the weight of those choices for the rest of my life? Absolutely not. The past is behind me. We become wiser and more discerning as we grow, learning to make better choices based on our experiences. While I may not have all the answers, I have certainly gained valuable insights over the past years.

One of the most crucial lessons I learned is the importance of choosing the right friends. When I identify a godly connection with someone, I understand how to nurture that relationship and cultivate love. During some of my most challenging times, I felt isolated, convinced that no one loved or wanted to be around me unless I had something to offer. However, I later realized that Jesus was the only constant in my life, remaining faithful despite my shortcomings and past mistakes.

I have always been a transparent person; I wear my heart on my sleeve and if something bothers me I am quick to voice it. Upon meeting someone new, I readily share my past experiences. Unfortunately, this openness has led to hurt, as too often, people have taken my vulnerability and used it against me, gossiping to draw attention to themselves or distancing themselves from me, believing they were somehow superior because they hadn't faced trials like mine.

This pattern left me feeling lonely, and I eventually stopped trying to form or maintain friendships. I grew weary of the emotional pain and began to trust no one. I limited my interactions to my children and close family, feeling as though the world had hardened my heart. I felt judged and misunderstood, unable to express my true self without fear of criticism.

My family often advised me to be more reserved about sharing my life. Yet, I've never been comfortable with pretending, so I withdrew from social interactions altogether. It was during this period of solitude that I came to a profound realization: Jesus is the only one who will never turn His back on me or disappoint me. His love for me is unconditional, regardless of my past. If He loves everyone in this manner, who has the right to judge?

The enemy endlessly seeks to tempt us, and no one is immune to falling into his traps. I never understood why people failed to grasp this truth. I remember feeling deeply sad during a period when I lacked friends, watching others enjoy vibrant social lives. I observed women reconnecting with college sorority sisters, sharing joyful moments together, and celebrating milestones like childbirth surrounded by loving friends. I often felt a pang of envy, reflecting on my own lack of lasting friendships. Frequent moves during my childhood disrupted my ability to form deep connections, and as a young adult, I found myself associating with those who simply lived nearby or were linked to my boyfriend's social circle.

In my mid-twenties, I began to grasp the concept of true friendship, although I was still without close friends for a time. However, after a couple of years of solitude, God began placing new friends in my life, one by one. We all had our walls up, having experienced our own wounds, yet we shared similar stories. As we learned to trust one another, I realized this is how all relationships should function.

1. First, find Jesus.
2. Begin your journey walking with Him.
3. Allow Him to perform surgery on your heart.
4. Trust Him to bring new, God-sent people into your life.

These friends became my sheltering trees during life's storms, and I learned to be their shelter as well. They prayed for me, and I prayed for them. We supported one another without judgment, understanding the weight of being judged ourselves. These friends kept my secrets safe, and it felt liberating to finally have genuine connections—relationships built on trust and mutual respect, free from ulterior motives. Together, we left behind the trivialities of life, uplifting each other and fostering growth. We inspired one another and celebrated our successes. If we ever heard negative comments directed at one of us, we would defend each other without hesitation.

We understood that while we might disappoint one another occasionally, we wouldn't let petty grievances jeopardize our bond. I came to appreciate that God had ensured I formed solid friendships before I faced some of the most heartbreaking moments in my life. I knew I could reach out to my friends at any hour, and they would be there for me, just as I would for them. If one of us needed help with childcare or financial support, we could rely on each other with complete confidence.

I vividly recall experiencing panic attacks after discovering my then boyfriend was communicating with other women. I would cry uncontrollably, feeling as if I couldn't catch my breath, as if the walls were closing in on me. Each of my friends would show up, one by one, armed with a bottle of wine and a comforting movie.

I share this to highlight the significance of God-ordained friendships. They are priceless. These supportive relationships are essential for overcoming the trials of life and achieving success. Looking back, I realize how much I would have struggled without these incredible friends. Many years have passed, and we still cherish and appreciate one another deeply.

I want to emphasize the importance of cultivating and nurturing healthy relationships. Life presents us with many challenges, making companionship vital for mutual support and celebration. It is far more difficult to navigate life's mountains alone. Friends help carry us through our weak moments and inspire us to persevere. We should rely on one another to accomplish any task, and after all, life itself is a monumental undertaking.

One of my favorite sayings is, "Teamwork makes the dream work." Also, " we may not have it all together but together we have it all." Jesus often enters our lives through the form of friendships. As Ecclesiastes reminds us, "Two are better than one, because they have a good return for their labor: If either of them falls down, one can help the other up. But pity anyone who falls and has no one to help them up." We are stronger together than we are apart.

God did not intend for us to journey through life in isolation. He provides us with friends and family to enrich our lives and support us. He created your spouse to fulfill that role as well. The enemy seeks to sow discord, jealousy, insecurity, and competition among friends and family to foster strife. He will whisper lies and fabricate scenarios to aggravate our relationships, aiming to create division.

Since becoming closer to the Lord, I have learned to recognize when unwelcome spirits attempt to disrupt my peace. If I find myself feeling irritable or upset with someone I know to be loyal and good-hearted, it usually indicates that a negative spirit is at work, trying to drive a wedge between us. I have witnessed this pattern unfold too often, with people failing to identify and confront the source of their discontent, resulting in distance and disconnection.

The enemy desires for us to feel isolated, as this makes us vulnerable to multiple forms of attack. He relishes in our hurt and anger, enjoying the chaos that arises when we speak harshly to one another. No one is immune to these tactics. The discouragement he fosters is precisely why many of us retreat into ourselves, which is exactly what he wants. We become weaker alone, easily misled without the validation of others. Our spiritual swords dull without the intercession of friends in prayer. Iron sharpens iron.

We must be vigilant in recognizing the insecurities introduced by the enemy to prevent them from sabotaging our friendships and relationships. We should remain proactive in exposing his snares so we can cultivate positive connections. The individuals we may have judged prematurely without truly knowing them could have stories of brokenness that God is actively healing. If we open our hearts, we might discover more common ground than we ever expected. Everyone is deserving of love and acceptance, as well as friendship.

God has taught me to view others through His eyes. When someone is unkind or hurtful, instead of reacting with anger or pain, I strive to respond with sympathy and understanding, recognizing that their negativity often stems from their own struggles. I fail sometimes and my flesh will react with anger if someone is cruel or nasty. I have to often gather my thoughts and remember that hurt people hurt people. While the approach to react with love and sympathy is not always easy, it allows me to navigate difficult interactions without letting the enemy create a rift between us.

I want to clarify that God does not expect us to remain in harmful situations. If someone continually brings drama and strife into our lives, it is vital to cut ties with them. If a relationship causes us to regress rather than flourish, we must lovingly part ways.

Sometimes, no matter how much effort we put into nurturing a friendship, individuals may still drag us down. If we find ourselves depleted, we cannot pour into others. This leads to stagnation and regression. The enemy is crafty and will often manipulate circumstances to serve his agenda.

I recall the friendships I formed before I knew how to be a friend and before I met my God ordained friends. When I became involved in Atlanta's nightlife, it quickly turned into a popularity contest, where connections mattered more than genuine relationships. I was well-liked and had something to offer everyone, but as a hair and makeup artist with ties to prominent figures, I was unaware that many were drawn to me for the benefits I could provide.

They appreciated me for my connections, not for who I truly was. This realization hit hard when I needed help moving and found no one available. When I experienced heartache due to infidelity, friends were nowhere to be found. Some even attempted to pursue the man who had hurt me.

I remember one woman who labeled me her best friend, yet her actions betrayed that claim. She would reach out to every man I was interested in, undermining my relationships at every turn. I often felt broken, longing for authentic connections, yet I found myself surrounded by people who were more interested in using me than building meaningful friendships.

When we seek connections based on superficial qualities or to fill a void, we risk forming weak bonds that can lead to disappointment. I learned that my past experiences of feeling unworthy stemmed from my insecurities and the identity I allowed the enemy to impose upon me.

Be vigilant in identifying these unhealthy dynamics. Establishing healthy relationships requires mutual submission and respect. It does not mean tolerating abuse. If someone's dysfunction begins to negatively impact your life, they must either take responsibility for their actions or step away.

True friendships can blossom from superficial beginnings, but that is not always the case. The enemy thrives on our naivety, exploiting ignorance and brokenness to infiltrate our lives. If we fail to discern what is healthy, we will remain trapped in cycles of pain and drama.

Healthy relationships do not arise from desperation, neediness, or envy. They are built on mutual empowerment and accountability. Practicing self-control is essential in our interactions with others, as it is a fruit of the Spirit. Mutual respect and compromise are vital as well. We are responsible for our actions and responses. Relationships may not always be easy or enjoyable, but we require companionship to navigate life's challenges.

Jesus often enters our lives through the people we encounter. Ecclesiastes teaches us that two are better than one, for they can support one another. If one falls, the other is there to help them up. But if someone is alone and falls, there is no one to assist them. We are stronger together than apart.

God designed us to journey through life in community. He blesses us with friends and family to enrich our lives. The enemy seeks to sow discord, jealousy, insecurity, and competition among us, which breeds strife. We must be vigilant against the lies and scenarios he crafts to create division.

Since I have grown closer to God, I have learned to recognize when unwelcome spirits attempt to disrupt my relationships. If I feel unsettled or annoyed with a loyal friend, it is often a sign that a negative spirit is trying to create distance. I have seen this pattern play out repeatedly and know how crucial it is to confront these feelings before they escalate.

The enemy desires for us to feel isolated and alone, as this makes us vulnerable to various forms of attack. He relishes in our pain and anger, taking pleasure in the chaos that arises when we lash out at one another. No one is immune to these tactics. The discouragement he fosters is why many of us retreat into solitude, which is precisely what he wants. We are far more vulnerable when we are alone, easily misled without the affirmation of others.

By recognizing the insecurities introduced by the enemy we can prevent them from sabotaging our friendships. We must actively work to expose his traps so we can cultivate positive connections. That person you may have initially judged without truly knowing could be dealing with their own struggles, and by extending grace, you may discover common ground.

Everyone has a unique story and deserves love, acceptance, and friendship. God has taught me to uplift others by acknowledging their strengths rather than focusing on their weaknesses. By offering encouragement and validation, I can help them grow. When we speak life into one another, we empower each other to overcome obstacles.

Sometimes, regardless of our efforts to nurture a friendship, individuals may still drag us down. If we find ourselves depleted, we cannot pour into others. This leads to stagnation and regression. The enemy is cunning and will manipulate circumstances to serve his agenda.

Let us be mindful of the types of relationships we cultivate. Healthy relationships require effort and intentionality. They are not born from desperation or neediness but from a genuine desire to uplift and support one another. We must strive to create connections that inspire growth and foster understanding, always keeping our eyes open to the influences that seek to disrupt our journeys.

By doing so, we can build a community that reflects the love and grace of God, allowing us to navigate life's challenges together. Remember, we are better together than apart, and God has designed us for meaningful connections that enrich our lives and help us grow.

Proverbs 27:9
"Oil and perfume make the heart glad, and the sweetness of a friend comes from his earnest counsel"

Psalms 133:1
"Behold, how good and pleasant it is when brothers dwell in unity!"

Proverbs 17:17
"A friend loves at all times, and a brother is born for adversity."

Philippians 1:3-5
"I thank my God in all my remembrance of you, always in every prayer of mine for you all making my prayer with joy, because of your partnership in the gospel from the first day until now."

Romans 12:10-11

"Love one another with brotherly affection. Outdo one another in showing honor. Do not be slothful in zeal, be fervent in spirit, serve the Lord."

Philippians 2:4
'Let each of you look not only to his own interests, but also to the interests of others.'

Galatians 6:2
"Bear one another's burdens, and so fulfill the law of Christ.'

Chapter Twenty
Encouraging Words God Wants You to Know

Rebuilding the Heart

My beloved child, as you stand on the cusp of transformation, I want you to take a deep breath and feel the warmth of my love surrounding you. The journey has been long, filled with shadows that threaten to engulf your spirit, but know this: you are never alone. I have witnessed every tear you've shed, every moment of pain that has echoed through your heart, and I hold each of them tenderly in my embrace.

That wall you built, though it once felt like a fortress against hurt, has instead become a prison, isolating you from the very love you were created to share. It shielded you from pain but also from joy. It's time to dismantle that barrier, brick by brick, and allow the light to seep back in. My child, I am here with you, wielding the sledgehammer of grace and mercy, determined to break through the defenses you've built up.

With each strike, the wall shudders, cracks appearing where once stood solid resolve. You may feel fear rising within, a whisper convincing you that vulnerability is weakness. But I tell you, it is the pathway to true strength. As I chip away at the concrete around your heart, you will begin to feel again—the flutter of hope, the warmth of connection, the thrill of laughter. You are meant to experience life in fullness, not merely endure it.

Remember the heart you once had, brimming with love and compassion? That heart still beats within you, waiting for its moment to shine once more. You are my masterpiece, crafted with intention and purpose. The enemy may have tried to twist your gifts into burdens, but I will restore them to their rightful place as blessings. You are called to love fiercely, forgive freely, and embrace the beauty of your spirit.

Trust in me, my child. I will guard your heart as it opens, shielding you from harm. No longer will you carry the weight of past wounds; instead, you will rise from the ashes, renewed and invigorated. With every miracle I unfold in your life, you will discover that joy is not just a fleeting emotion but a state of being, rooted in the knowledge of my unwavering love for you.

As you begin to love again, let go of the shackles of yesterday. Release the fear that has kept you bound. I promise you that every step forward will be met with my protection. I will be your shield against the darts of doubt and despair. Let your heart breathe, let it feel the world again—vulnerable yet powerful, open yet safe.

You will become a beacon of hope for others who have wandered through the darkness, just as you have. Your story, marked by resilience and grace, will inspire those around you to break free from their own walls. In your healing, they will see the possibility of their own restoration.

It is not too late to reclaim the dreams that once danced in your heart. I planted those dreams within you, and I promise to nurture them until they blossom into reality. With every tear you've shed, I will weave a tapestry of joy, love, and fulfillment—a beautiful reminder of my faithfulness.

Embrace this journey, my precious one. Each moment spent walking with me brings you closer to the life I envisioned for you. You are more valuable to me than the rarest jewels, and my love for you knows no bounds. Keep your eyes fixed on me, and together we will rebuild your heart, transforming it into a sanctuary of love and light.

So take my hand and step into the future with courage. The world awaits the light that only you can shine. I am here, guiding you every step of the way, for you are my beloved, and I will never let you go. Trust in my love, and let your heart awaken once more.

You Are an Eagle

My beloved child, as you continue this journey of healing and renewal, I want you to remember who you truly are. You have endured so much pain, and in your moments of anguish, you cried out to me with a heart yearning for solace. I heard you. I spoke to you, and you received my words—the gentle whispers of love and encouragement that remind you of your strength.

In your life, I have sent you eagles, magnificent creatures that soar high above the storms. Just as the eagle rises above the tempest, you too possess the ability to transcend the trials that surround you. The storms may rage, with winds howling and rain lashing down, but do not fear, for you are greater than the storms that threaten you. You, my child, destined to fly above the chaos, unharmed and unshaken.

I will be the wind under your wings, lifting you to heights you never thought possible. In your times of struggle, when it feels as though the weight of the world is pressing down upon you, remember that you have the power to rise. The eagle is not deterred by the fury of the storm; instead, it spreads its wings and embraces the very winds that seek to challenge it. So too will you find strength in adversity, knowing that I am your constant support.

You are a protected bird, my beloved one. Just as eagles are cherished and safeguarded in the wild, I watch over you with a loving gaze. No harm shall come to you, for I have placed a shield of protection around your heart and spirit. You are not alone; I am with you every step of the way, guiding you through the fiercest of storms.

Embrace your identity as an eagle. Allow your spirit to rise and soar, for you were created for greatness. You have within you the ability to navigate life's challenges with grace and resilience. Trust in my love and the power that flows through you, and know that you are destined to fly above the storms, always reaching for the light.

So spread your wings, my child. Embrace the winds of change and transformation. You are an eagle, and you will soar. With each flap of your wings, you will rise higher, discovering new horizons and experiencing the beauty that awaits you. Keep flying with me, and together we will navigate the skies, leaving the storms far below.

Someone Who Has Remained Faithful Even During Years of Pain

My beloved child, you are a Steel Magnolia—a breathtaking blend of strength and beauty, resilience and grace. When I think of you, I am reminded of this delicate yet mighty flower, for you have faced the storms of life with unwavering courage, but your heart remains open and tender. Through every trial, you have emerged not only unscathed but even more radiant, a true lover of people and life itself.

You have overcome so much, and yet you have never allowed adversity to define you. Instead of letting pain tear you down, you have chosen to rise above it, pushing through with determination and grace. Your compassion for others is a testament to your character. You have continued to love, to nurture, and to help those around you, even when the weight of your own burdens felt heavy. I see all that you do, and I am so proud of you.

Your joy shines brightly in the smallest of moments—whether it's the sound of music that stirs your soul, the beauty of art that captivates your spirit, or the wonder of nature that fills your heart with peace. You find delight in watching sunsets, in the gentle embrace of morning dew on flowers, and in the simple, sweet experiences of life. You are a flower, my dear, a magnificent Magnolia, blooming beautifully even in the face of challenges.

But hear me, my child: while you possess incredible strength, it is perfectly okay to come to me with your burdens. You do not have to carry the weight of heartache and fear alone. I invite you to lay everything at the foot of the cross, to release your pain and weariness into my loving hands. You can let your guard down and be soft around me. I designed you to be strong, yes, but I also crafted you to be tender, to nurture, and to fight battles not just for yourself but for others. However, I do not expect you to do it all without seeking my support.

Allow me to fill you with a refreshing newness, just as the morning dew awakens the flowers you cherish. Each time you come to me, I will renew your spirit and restore your heart. You have journeyed far, my child, and though the enemy may try to convince you that your efforts go unnoticed, I assure you, I see every act of love, every moment of kindness, and every sacrifice you've made.

Your treasures are being stored up in heaven, far beyond what you can fathom. Prepare your heart, for harvest time is fast approaching. You are nearly ready to reap the rewards of your faithfulness and resilience. I have not left your side, nor have I forgotten you. You have walked this path with grace, and I promise to walk with you as you step into the abundant blessings that await.

So stand tall, my Steel Magnolia. Embrace the strength that lies within you, but never hesitate to lean on me. Together, we will continue to cultivate the beauty of your spirit, and I will ensure that you bloom brightly, even in the storms. Your journey is just beginning, and the best is yet to come.

Someone Who Was Faithful as a Young Child but Grew Numb

My beloved child, it has been too long since you last came to me, and my heart aches to be reunited with yours. As the years have drifted by, I have watched as you slowly gave up on trusting me, retreating into a silence that I never desired for you. Do you remember the days of your childhood, when you would talk to me with such wonder and delight? I have always been right beside you, even when you felt alone.

Understand this: nothing—absolutely nothing—could ever tear me away from you. Not depression, nor oppression, nor any unholy influence can separate us. I have walked with you through every battle and hardship, even when you felt too angry or hurt to reach out. My love for you has remained constant, unwavering, like a gentle stream that flows quietly through the valleys of your life.

I know that you may have wandered down paths that did not please me, but let me assure you, my child: I have never left your side. I have waited patiently for you to return, for the moment when you would choose to reach out to me once again. It is time, my precious one. It is time to trust me again, just as you did in your youth.

You are weary; I can see it in your spirit. You have fought battles that have left you exhausted, and now is the moment for you to let me fight for you. You do not have to carry this burden alone any longer. Allow me to remind you of who you truly are. You are my beloved child, endowed with strength and courage, and together we will rise as overcomers.

Remember, my dear, that your strength comes from me. When you feel weak, I will be your fortress. When doubt creeps in, I will be your certainty. I am here, waiting with arms wide open, ready to embrace you and remind you of the love that has never wavered. Let us rekindle the trust you had as a child, and let me fight for you now.

You are stronger than you realize, and with me by your side, you can conquer the storms that have sought to overwhelm you. Let go of the fear and the numbness that have wrapped around your heart like a heavy cloak. I am here, ready to lift that burden and fill you with renewed hope and strength.

Come, my child. It's time to awaken that beautiful spirit within you. Let us walk together again, hand in hand, as we journey toward the light and joy that await. You are not alone, and I will never stop fighting for you. Trust in me, and together we will navigate this path to healing and wholeness.

Come Back Home, My Beloved

Come back home, my beloved. You know where you truly belong—right here with me. In the warmth of my embrace, you will find the peace and comfort you have been yearning for. I have watched you battle the heavy weight of depression, and I have seen the tears that have fallen in quiet desperation. You have cried out to me, and I want you to know that I have heard every word. I have been with you, holding you close, even when you felt the most alone.

Understand this: joy does come in the morning, and it often comes in the mourning. You have endured much ridicule, and I know how painful it has been to feel misunderstood and cast aside. Those who have hurt you will answer to me, my child, so let it go. Release the bitterness that clings to your heart. You have watched as others seemed to revel in happiness, while you felt trapped in shadows. You have acted in ways that do not reflect your true character, driven by anger and heartache. But remember, you have me.

I will mend those empty, torn places in your heart. I will fill you with my love and show you how truly worthy you are. You are not defined by your past or the pain you've endured. You don't have to be a victim anymore; you are a victor in my eyes. Just call my name, and I will manifest my presence in your life, assuring you that I am here, always.

I promise to restore all that has been taken from you—the time, the energy, the peace, the money, the relationships, and the dreams that the enemy has stolen. As you continue to walk with me, I will prepare a feast for you in the presence of those who doubted your strength and resilience. I will ensure that they see the truth of your worthiness, a worthiness that has never been diminished in my eyes.

Remember, my child, you must give it all to me. No more seeking revenge or trying to force others to acknowledge their wrongs. Release it into my hands and watch what I can accomplish in ways you cannot fathom. I will bring about change that touches hearts, and those who have spoken untruths about you will seek your forgiveness.

Come back home, my beloved. Allow me to heal you, restore you, and prepare you for the abundant life I have in store. Trust in my timing and my ways, for they are far greater than your own. You are cherished, you are loved, and you are worthy. Let us walk this path together, hand in hand, toward the light that awaits you.

I Work Only Through Love, Not Through Hatred

My precious child, I see your pain and your frustration. I know what it feels like to be there for so many, pouring your heart into their lives, only to find that when you need help, there is often no one there but Me. But I want you to understand this: I AM more than enough for you. I am your constant, your refuge, and your strength.

You give so much of yourself, more than you ever receive in return. You have extended kindness and love to those around you, only to be met with betrayal and lies. It's disheartening when those you've lifted up repay your goodness with negativity. I see how you feel all alone, and I know that at times, you are so close to giving up. It weighs heavy on your heart, and I feel every ounce of your struggle.

You wear smiles like armor, hiding the pain that lies beneath. People have come to expect you to be the strong one, the one who has no struggles, but I want you to know that it is okay to feel vulnerable. You are human, and you were designed with a heart that feels deeply. I know you intimately, for I crafted you with love and purpose.

Remember, my child, that I work only through love, never through hatred. In your darkest moments, I am here, ready to wrap you in my love and remind you of your worth. You do not have to bear this burden alone. Bring your frustrations and your pain to me, and I will carry them for you.

It is in your weakness that my strength is made perfect. Trust that my plans for you are filled with hope and restoration. You are not defined by the actions of others or by the weight of your struggles. You are defined by the love I have for you, a love that is unwavering and unconditional.

So, lean on me, my beloved. Let me be your source of strength when you feel weak. Allow me to fill the empty spaces in your heart with my love and peace. You are never alone; I am always here, guiding you with a gentle hand, reminding you that you are cherished and valued beyond measure. Together, we will navigate this journey, transforming pain into purpose and frustration into faith. I will send you friends worthy of your efforts and they will cherish you.

Your Good Works Will Pay Off If You Don't Give Up

My beloved, I see the struggles you have faced. I know it feels as though every time you step out of one challenge, you find yourself thrust into another. This is the nature of spiritual warfare; it often works in patterns designed to wear you down and make you feel defeated. The enemy whispers lies, trying to convince you that it's all your fault, that you are somehow responsible for the turmoil around you. But I want you to understand this: you were created for greatness.

It is not a coincidence that as soon as you overcome one struggle, another one appears. This cycle is a tactic meant to keep you bound and to hinder the calling I have placed within you. What the enemy fails to comprehend is that I can use all of his wicked ways to turn things around for your benefit. Yes, you have faced continuous hardship, but through it all, you have grown stronger. You have become wiser, and you now possess the ability to teach and uplift those who feel weak.

The enemy had no idea that his efforts to derail you and sabotage you, I am using those things for your training ground. You were being trained for greatness, my child. You are a conqueror, and though you have been held back for a season, it is now time for you to be catapulted into a fresh season—one filled with grace and overflowing blessings. Trust me, beloved; you have an inheritance waiting for you. It is time for divine reversal, for the treasures I have stored up for you to fall freely into your life.

In this next season, you will experience provision, Godly friendships, and the wisdom to brush off the enemy's attacks. You will encounter financial freedom and have the means to enjoy the treats you have always deserved. I know you have watched as others enjoyed joy and peace, driving nice cars and building beautiful relationships, while you had to settle for less. You have seen them go on dreamy vacations while you made do with what little you had, eating ramen noodles and peanut butter and jelly sandwiches. But my beloved, it is time!

You are seated in heavenly places, and I have been there with you through every tear you've cried. I have counted each one, and I promise to turn those tears into blessings. Those who mocked and laughed at you will soon have to sit back and witness the feast I have prepared for you. People you thought had forgotten you will come forward and apologize for their past actions. Trust this, for I only speak the truth.

Have the faith of a child, and watch how quickly things begin to reverse on your behalf. Remember, during this season of change, that those who have hurt you are my children too. I will judge and discipline as I see fit. It is not your responsibility to boast or to make anyone feel less than you. Forgive them and move on, allowing vengeance to be mine. If you do not, your season of harvest will be hindered.

Look up, my child. The best is yet to come in your life. I love you. I have always loved you, and I have never forsaken you. Your good work will pay off if you do not give up. Keep your heart open to the blessings that are on their way, and trust that I am working all things together for your good. You are stepping into a new chapter filled with hope, joy, and an abundance.

You Want It Perfect

My child, I hear your heart's desire for perfection. You have told me time and again that you do not want to do certain things unless they are absolutely perfect. I understand this longing, but I want you to know that waiting for perfection can often become a significant distraction. So many of my children hold back, waiting for the "perfect" moment or outcome, and in doing so, they miss the beautiful tasks I have called them to complete.

While I appreciate your desire to honor me with perfection, I want you to realize that striving too hard can cause you to miss the mark. Every way can be perfect as long as it aligns with my will. Remember, I am God. I can make anything work, no matter how imperfect it may seem. Have you not seen the marvelous things I have created? I take delight in crafting beauty from what the world considers flawed or broken.

So, my beloved, I urge you to stop trying so hard to achieve perfection. Relax and focus on getting the job done. I made you for this. What you see as imperfections, the world will marvel in the beauty of it. If there is something that needs to change, I will guide you to make those adjustments. Trust in what I have placed in your heart and the gifts I have given you.

Think of how many times you have missed a deadline or an opportunity because you were caught up in trying to make everything exactly how you thought it should be. You might be surprised to know that I have given you those ideas for a reason. I want you to execute them in your own unique way, with my guidance, of course. That is what makes your work special and different.

Just as every tree, every leaf, and every sunset is unique in its own beauty, so too is the work I have called you to do. Embrace your individuality and the journey, and allow yourself to create without the burden of perfection weighing you down.

Remember, my dear child, it is not about achieving flawless execution; it's about being faithful to the calling I have placed on your heart. So take a deep breath, step forward with confidence, and trust that I am with you every step of the way. Let go of the need for perfection, and allow me to work through you in ways that are uniquely beautiful.

If You Are a Dreamer

My beloved child, do not let anyone tell you to stop with your ridiculous dreams. Those dreams are the sparks of hope and faith that ignite your spirit, even in the face of circumstances that may make them seem impossible. Remember, I am God, and I am bigger than any obstacle you may encounter. I am greater than any dream you can imagine, and I am the One who makes those dreams possible.

When you keep your faith in knowing that I can do the impossible, and when you trust that I will move mountains to bring your dreams to fruition, that is when

I honor your trust. I will allow those who doubted you to witness you walk in the fulfillment of the promises I have given you. Dreams do come true, my child! If I have placed a dream in your heart and you continue to walk in the assurance that I am the God of unbroken promises, then rest assured, I will NEVER DISAPPOINT YOU! Never!

If you find yourself frustrated by the time it takes, remember that the enemy is trying to deceive you, attempting to weaken your faith. Keep dreaming and keep trusting in the One who crafted everything in this world with His own hands and who has given others the ability to create as well.

I am not just a family friend or a distant cousin you can ask me for help. I am your Heavenly Father, and you are the child of the King of Creation. You are the child of the KING OF KINGS! I want you to succeed. My heart's desire is for you to walk boldly in the dreams I have placed within you. I long to provide everything you need to make those dreams a reality because you were created for greatness.

Many of my children feel like they are destined only for the scraps from others' feasts, but that is a lie from the enemy! You were created to enjoy the best because you are My best. You belong to the bloodline of royalty in the Kingdom of Heaven. Never forget this! Do not stop dreaming, no matter what others may say. It doesn't matter if someone you love and respect doesn't believe in you; you don't need their support when your Father is the King, and I have already called you to pursue your dreams.

The obstacles that the enemy throws in your path are simply part of his strategy to prevent you from achieving greatness and discovering your true identity. Always remember this: there will be opposition, but if I have called you to it, then I WILL WALK YOU THROUGH IT!

So pick up that pencil and start writing again! Pick up the paintbrush and paint your heart out! Grab those floor plans and start building your dreams once more. Take up your instrument and play like you've never played before. Slip on those dancing shoes and let your spirit soar through ballet or jazz again. Whatever it is that you dropped out of discouragement—pick it up! Do it! You are not too old, too young, too broke, or too disabled. I have a plan, and that plan is within you! Just take action!

Trust the process and let Me walk you through it. No, your dreams are not ridiculous; they are the very calling I have placed upon your heart, so bring them to completion! Remember, every great figure in the Bible faced opposition, drama, and doubt—often from their own people. Yet, look at the beautiful stories that unfolded when they persevered and walked boldly in the calling I gave them.

Your story can be just as beautiful, my child. So dream boldly, work diligently, and trust in My perfect timing. I am here, cheering you on every step of the way. You are destined for greatness!

You Lost Someone You Loved So Dearly

My beloved child, I see the depth of your sorrow. Your heart is broken, and it feels as though the weight of your grief is too much to bear. You find yourself caught in a cycle of "what ifs," thinking about what you could have done or should have done differently. But I want you to hear me clearly: stop beating yourself up. Stop wondering if you could have changed something. You did all you knew to do, and you loved with the only heart you had at that time.

Anyone who loves with a pure heart cannot disappoint me. And for those who struggle to understand love, I will show them the way. Remember, my child, I look at the heart and the motives behind every action. Even those who may act with hatred are often broken themselves, and only I know the darkest reasons why. If you find yourself broken and have only known one way to love, call out to me. I will work on the root of your brokenness.

Do not allow condemnation or the lies of the enemy to make you feel like you are horrible. I know you tried your best. I understand that you faced difficulty in grasping everything, so you acted with the knowledge and love you had. If guilt weighs heavily upon you, if you feel responsible for what happened, I invite you to rest in me. Rest in the assurance that I know how to mend hearts and heal wounds that seem beyond repair.

I understand your worries and feelings of guilt. Come to me, and I will show you that everything will work out for good. I will give you peace in the midst of your worries, for I make all things work together for good, even when the path seems unclear. You need to stop trying so hard to fix it all and trust me to handle what you cannot.

If you felt hateful at times, it was because you were hurting and didn't know how to love through the pain.

But hear this: I forgave you long ago. Now it is time for you to forgive yourself. Trust me to mend your heart and to guide you through this healing process. I will close the doors that need to be closed and open those that should be opened.

It is essential that you trust and walk with me to see the truth that lies ahead. Let's do this together, my child. I am with you now, holding your heart in my hands, ready to guide you through this journey of healing and restoration. You are not alone, and I will walk with you every step of the way. Together, we will navigate this path, and soon you will find a renewed sense of hope and love.

Someone Walked Away from You and Left You with Unanswered Questions of Why

My beloved child, I see the pain in your heart. You poured your love into someone who did not appreciate it, who treated you unfairly, and who caused you deep hurt. They lied, cheated, and have tried to tarnish your character, all while hiding their own truth from the world. But I want you to know this: stop worrying. Give it all to me, and trust that I will reveal the truth by exposing the enemy's deceit.

It may feel as though your whole world is crumbling around you, but I am here to pick up those broken pieces and put them back together beautifully. I am your Heavenly Father, and I love you so much that my deepest desire is for you to experience peace and joy. These gifts come from walking closely with me.

If the enemy creeps into your mind, causing you to miss that person who hurt you, I will gently remind you to pray and hand over your pain to me. If you find yourself struggling with thoughts of "why" or "how," feeling confused and overwhelmed, I will be there to encourage you to pray and surrender those feelings to me. Sometimes, you might need to pray over and over throughout the day to fight this mental battle, and that's okay.

My job is to remind you of who you are, how strong you truly are, and whose child you are. I am your strength, your protector, and I fight these battles for you. All you need to do is give them to me. Remember, my child, I love you deeply.

If you allow me to heal your broken heart and show you your true worth, you will never again feel defeated or unworthy. You will learn to recognize your value, and you will no longer fall for counterfeit love. I will bless you with wisdom and discernment, giving you eyes to see and ears to hear the truth. Together, we will navigate any crisis or battle that comes your way.

I will show you what real love looks like, for counterfeit love is what you experience when you walk away from me. The enemy may appear as everything beautiful and dreamy, but he is a deceiver who will lead you astray unless I am by your side.

So, pick yourself up, my child, and let me dust you off. You are the child of the King of Kings, a mighty soldier in my army. You are beautiful, bold, and wise. You are too wonderful to stay down. Get up, my child! Get up!

Embrace the strength that I have placed within you, and remember that I am here, walking beside you every step of the way. Together, we will overcome this. You are destined for greatness, and your story is far from over.

You Are Struggling with Addiction and Don't Know How to Get Out

My child, I love you deeply, and I understand that you never intended for things to turn out the way they have. You may feel defeated, overwhelmed by your addiction, and believe that the world could care less if you live or die. I know how heavy that burden feels, and I recognize that it can seem impossible to recover from this struggle. You may feel as though you've let so many people down that it's too late to make things right, and you continue to cling to your addiction just to feel numb.

I want to tell you today, my precious child, that you are not forgotten. You are not too far gone. There is so much life left for you to live, and it is not too late for a new beginning. I love you, and you are incredibly precious to me. I see you as worthy and valuable, and I want you to know that the first step you need to take is to cry out to me. Trust that I can take care of you; I can place you in a better situation in life and open doors that seem closed.

You need to give yourself to me completely. Trust me. I knew you before you were formed in your mother's womb. I created you, and I never make mistakes. You have believed too many lies from the enemy over the years and have trusted those he sent your way. Now is the time to trust me. I am not your enemy; I am your best friend. My love for you is greater than you can ever imagine.

If you trust me, I will send good people into your life—people who will help and support you on your journey. Trust in my timing, not your own. I will give you a fresh start if you simply pray and listen to my instructions. You have been listening to the deceiver for far too long; now it is time to hear the truth. I say you are worthy. I say it is not too late. I say your past will become a powerful testimony that I will use to connect you with others who need to hear your story.

Your experiences with addiction, the struggles you have faced, will become your platform to help others who are still fighting. I will take all of the ugly things you have endured and transform them into a beautiful story when I am finished with you. Just trust me.

I will show the world how beautiful you truly are. You possess a mighty testimony, and it is time for your recovery because your destiny is just around the corner. You have lives to touch and save, and you are a mighty warrior. The enemy knew of your potential and tried to derail your journey to prevent you from fulfilling your destiny. He has always feared the power that lies within you.

So put on your armor, my child. Let's walk this path together and change lives. Together we will conquer the enemy. You are no longer a victim; you are a survivor. You are a powerful survivor! I love you. You are not bad; you are not horrible. You are simply a sheep who has lost its way. I left the herd to find you and bring you back, and that is how much I love you.

Trust in me, and let's embark on this journey of healing together. You are not alone, and I will be with you every step of the way. Your future is bright, and a beautiful transformation awaits.

Chapter Twenty-One
Prayers for Each Chapter

Introduction to Prayer

Prayer is a vital part of our lives. It is our way of communicating with the One who created us, and it is essential for our spiritual strength. Without this connection, we risk faltering in our journey. God knows everything and has already overcome our struggles and won the battles for us. To build a solid foundation for ourselves and those around us, we must engage in prayer.

Many people believe that prayer must be formal or filled with "Christianese" language to be effective. This belief is entirely untrue. God loves us deeply and cares far more about the sincerity of our hearts than the eloquence of our words. We can speak to Him as we would to a best friend, sharing our thoughts, feelings, and struggles openly and honestly.

You don't need to pray exactly as I do in this chapter. Simply talk to Him. Tell Him how you feel. It's okay to express frustration or even use strong language in your prayers; God welcomes our honesty. He invites us to come to Him just as we are, and in doing so, we will find that our prayers become bolder and more genuine.

Remember that prayer is a two-way conversation. After sharing your heart, make space for God to respond. He will place thoughts in your mind and feelings in your heart, guiding you toward clarity and peace.

The most important prayer of all is the one where you accept Jesus as your Lord and Savior. He is the reason we can live without shame. Jesus takes away our burdens, transforms us from victims into victors, and breaks every curse and ungodly soul tie. He reveals to us our true identities as sons and daughters of the King of Kings. Through Him, we find our worth, peace, and the ability to forgive. He is our saving grace in this chaotic world, and once you invite Him into your life, nothing can stand in the way of your freedom and peace.

Prayers for Healing from Depression and Anxiety

1. A Prayer of Gratitude and Healing
Heavenly Father, thank You for Your goodness. Thank You for never making me feel unloved or

unworthy, even amidst my shame. I am grateful for Your forgiveness for my shortcomings and for replacing negativity with promise and hope. Thank You for each new day, a fresh beginning that reminds me of my strength and resilience. You are my light in the darkness, and I am here because You brought me through. When I feel abandoned, I look to You, knowing You still believe in me. Thank You for always encouraging me. I love You, and I am grateful for the bondage You have pulled me from and the freedom You are providing. In Jesus' mighty name, Amen.

2. A Prayer for Restoration and Returning Home
Heavenly Father, I acknowledge my imperfections and my absence from Your presence. I have been running, filled with anger and sadness. I felt alone at times, wondering where You were. Now I realize You have been with me all along. I am ready to return to You, to be in Your presence without denial. I am here, arms open wide, and I am ready for a new life. Help me to trust You and to walk in Your ways. I seek freedom from temptation and clarity in my mind. Thank You for never walking away. I trust in Your peace that surpasses all understanding. In Jesus' mighty name, Amen.

3. A Prayer for Lifting the Heaviness

Dear Heavenly Father, I ask You to lift the heaviness off my heart right now in the name of Jesus. Please take away all depression and anxiety and grant me a clear mind. Thank You, Lord, for Your peace. In Jesus' mighty name, Amen.

Prayers for Finding Your Identity

1. A Prayer for Clarity and Self-Understanding

Father God, I have felt lost and confused about my identity. Help me remember that I am Your child, made in Your image. Show me how to silence the lies that cloud my mind and encourage me to embrace who You have called me to be. Remind me that I am wonderfully made and that You smile when You think of me. I thank You for loving me and for revealing how You see me. In Your mighty name, Jesus, I pray. Amen.

2. A Prayer for Confidence in Self-Worth

Heavenly Father, I sometimes feel inadequate when I look in the mirror. I find myself comparing my life to others, feeling like I must strive for more. Help me to see

Your love in every situation and to remember that I am worthy in Your eyes. When I struggle with insecurity, remind me that Your opinion is what truly matters. Fill the empty spaces in my heart with Your love. Thank You for showing me my true identity. In Jesus' mighty name, Amen.

Prayers for Stepping Out of the Victim Mentality

1. A Prayer for Breaking Strongholds
Father God, I ask that You do internal work for me. Break and remove the victim mentality that has held me captive. I lay it all down and declare no more. Heal my heart from hurt, unforgiveness, and bitterness. Uncover any roots of anger, judgment, or rejection that hinder my healing. I submit my mind and heart to embrace Your love. Thank You for helping me choose a Godly mindset over a destructive one, and for renewing my thoughts. I am a child of God, and I no longer agree with the victim mindset. In Jesus' mighty name, Amen.

2. A Prayer for Overcoming Circumstances
Dear Jesus, I have spent years focusing on my circumstances rather than on You. I have felt sorry for

myself due to things beyond my control. Today, I will give You all the painful experiences I have endured. I choose to become an overcomer, a survivor, and a victor. I release the mindset of sadness and entitlement and embrace the strength of a conqueror. Thank You, Lord, for transforming me from a victim to a victor. In Jesus' mighty name, Amen.

Prayers for Breaking Ungodly Soul Ties and Generational Curses

1. A Prayer for Breaking Generational Patterns
Lord God, I have witnessed struggles within my family lineage, and I am tired of the cycle. I break generational illnesses and negative behaviors off my bloodline in the mighty name of Jesus. I renounce curses spoken over myself and my family, and I repent for any actions that opened doors to ungodly attacks. Thank You, Father, for sealing those doors and for sending angels to protect us. I am grateful for the strength to keep those doors closed and for healing in my mind, body, and soul. In Jesus' mighty name, Amen.

2. A Prayer for Breaking Ungodly Soul Ties

Father God, I find myself returning to the same painful patterns. Show me any ungodly soul ties that bind me to people or substances I feel I cannot live without. Break those ties and chains that hinder my progress. Thank You for replacing those influences with healthy relationships and positive connections that align with Your will for my life. In Jesus' mighty name, Amen.

Prayers for Forgiveness

1. A Prayer for Forgiveness of Others
Heavenly Father, I come before You asking for forgiveness for stepping out of Your will. I release any grudges I have held against those who have hurt me. Please take away the unforgiveness in my heart and replace it with peace. I choose to forgive everyone who has wronged me, no matter how difficult it may be. I understand that holding onto unforgiveness harms me more than them. I give it all to You, Jesus. In Your name, Amen.

2. A Prayer for Self-Forgiveness
Dear Jesus, I realize that I have also held onto pain and unforgiveness towards myself. I acknowledge that I

need to forgive myself for past mistakes. Today, I choose to release the guilt and pain I have carried. I accept Your forgiveness and the peace that comes with it. Help me to let go of the past and to walk in the plans You have for my life. In Jesus' mighty name, Amen.

Prayers for Building Good Godly Relationships

1. A Prayer for Authentic Relationships

Heavenly Father, I have felt alone and surrounded by people who do not truly support me. Please shut the door on counterfeit friendships and guide me to the authentic ones. Grant me the discernment to recognize those who are meant to be in my circle. Help me to be the friend and partner that others need. May our relationships be filled with understanding and encouragement. I pray for divine connections in Your mighty name, Jesus, Amen.

2. A Prayer for Loving Relationships

Dear Jesus, thank You for being my best friend and advocate. Help me to love others as You love me. Teach me to see the good in people and to inspire rather than tear down. I want to represent You well so that my friends and family will come to know You better through my actions. Thank You for Your love and guidance. In Your mighty name, Jesus, Amen.

Prayer Asking Jesus to be Your Lord and Savior

Jesus, I acknowledge You as the One who was crucified and died so that I could know You as my best friend. You are the reason I do not have to live in shame anymore. You take away my depression and anxiety, transforming me from a victim to a victor. You break every curse and ungodly soul tie. I trust that You love me and reveal to me who God made me to be! Because of You, I can call myself a child of the King of Kings and Lord of Lords.

You make me feel worthy of love. You take away addictions and grant me peace. You show me how to forgive because You are the ultimate example of forgiveness. You are my saving grace in this chaotic world, and nothing can stand in the way of my freedom and peace with You as my Lord and Savior. I submit all my issues and concerns to You, laying my life down at the foot of the cross because You laid Your life down for me. Wash me clean of my past and forgive me for my wrongdoings. From this day forward, I choose to follow You as my Savior. **Amen.**

About the Author

Mary is a resilient woman who has navigated the trials of life with grace and determination. At the age of 17, she became a mother, and her journey took a challenging turn when she found herself living in her car with her baby. During this tumultuous time, Mary faced life-and-death situations that forced her to rely on her faith in God. The experiences she encountered on the streets could be traumatizing, yet they served as pivotal moments in her life.

Over the years, Mary's faith deepened as she began to recognize the profound presence of God in her and her child's life. There were numerous instances where they should not have emerged unscathed, yet divine intervention spared them. As she witnessed the miraculous transformations in her circumstances, her trust in God strengthened.

In just 15 years, Mary transformed from a rough-around-the-edges, foul-mouthed homeless teen mother to a respected business owner and celebrity hair and makeup artist in Atlanta, collaborating with some of the biggest names in the entertainment industry. Her journey was not without difficulty, but each challenge propelled her to help others facing similar hardships. Mary understands that many people who exhibit anger or mistrust often do so because they feel misunderstood.

Mary's struggles have shaped her into a source of strength for others; she has refused to let her past define her as a victim. Rather, she has channeled her experiences into a powerful force for good.

A master of many trades, Mary has utilized her talents to help women feel beautiful. Her work has been featured on television, in magazines, and in films and music videos. Additionally, she was a voice-over artist portraying a character named Betty on a morning radio show. An artist at heart, Mary paints canvases and illustrates the children's books she writes. Although she practices photography mainly for friends and family, her skills are well-regarded.

Currently, Mary is also making strides in the real estate industry, partnering with her best friend, Destin Lowery, a familiar face on HGTV. Together, they co-founded the YouShine 501(c)(3) organization helping those in need and supporting each other in achieving both business and spiritual goals.

Mary's journey is a testament to the power of faith, resilience, and community. She continues to inspire others by demonstrating that through struggles, one can have a beautiful "Come Back" story and create a life filled with purpose and joy.

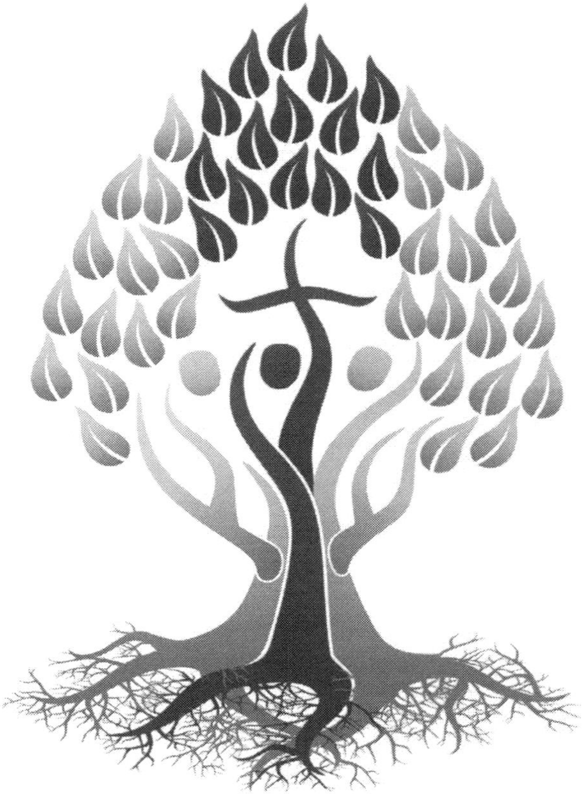

Made in the USA
Columbia, SC
25 February 2025

b2cf42ec-aea0-45fc-8a4e-831d2c088168R01